How to start kart racing

2002 Edition

Produced for the
Association
of
Racing Karts
Schools

ABkC

In conjunction with the
Association of British
Kart Clubs

t*f*m

Publishing
Limited

Published by TFM Publishing Ltd
Brimstree View
Kemberton
Shifnal
Shropshire
TF11 9LL

Tel: 01952 586408
Fax: 01952 587654
e-mail: nikki@tfmpub.freeserve.co.uk
Web site: www.tfmpublishing.co.uk

Design and layout: Nikki Bramhill
Photography: Chris Walker (01522 810271)

First edition December 1998
Second edition December 1999
Third edition December 2000
Fourth edition December 2001

ISBN 1 903378 07 9

CHAPTER 1
THE FIRST STEPS

IN THIS CHAPTER

1.1 THE BIG PICTURE

➤ A run down on the structure of kart racing both world-wide and in the UK.

➤ The role of the Motor Sports Association (MSA).

➤ The major international classes.

➤ The depth of the sport in Britain.

➤ Categories of race meetings.

1.2 THE ASSOCIATION OF RACING KART SCHOOLS

➤ The role of ARKS

➤ Member schools

➤ Instructor licensing

1.3 BACK TO SCHOOL

➤ What the schools offer

➤ The first lesson

➤ Racing with a school

1.4 CHOOSING A SCHOOL

➤ The ARKS standard

1.1 THE BIG PICTURE

Beware. Motor sport can be addictive. It has often been said that the sport should carry a government health warning. Once hooked, participants, be they racers, team members, officials or fans, can find it very difficult to escape the clutches of a sport that can take you from the heights of exhilaration to the depths of despair. Sometimes in the space of a few minutes. But, it is a great sport that provides excitement for thousands. If you are ultimately fortunate enough to compete, you will remember your racing for the rest of your life.

Globally, all motorsport is governed by the FIA (Federation Internationale de l'Automobile) from its office in Geneva. The responsibility for governing the sport nationally is devolved to individual bodies in each country. For the United Kingdom, it is the Motor Sports Association, commonly known as the MSA. Until the RAC was sold, it held this function and devolved the duties to the MSA but now the FIA recognises the MSA directly. Kart racing has its own international body - the CIK, or Commission Internationale de Karting, which is part of the FIA and based at their Swiss office. This body sets the international class regulations and organises the European and World Kart Championships.

The MSA is responsible for all aspects of regulation of motor sport. Its duties and powers are extensive and cover things like licensing of competitors, inspection and licensing of venues, control of technical regulations for karts and other vehicles and monitoring the organisation and running of events. With wide-ranging powers, the MSA is a professional body committed to the cause of ever-safer competition and the protection of the sport. Its revenue is largely generated from the licence fees paid by competitors.

While the MSA is concerned with the overall control of the sport, the promotion of kart racing in Britain rests with the kart clubs and associations. There are a number of relationships between the circuit owners and organising clubs but, ultimately, all are working towards more participants and larger crowds. Recent initiatives include lowering the starting age for competitors in some disciplines. These are subjects we will expand on in later chapters.

To set the scene, let's start at the top. At the pinnacle of world karting is Formula Super A (100cc), where the very best drivers in the sport compete for the biggest prize of all, the World crown. Top kart teams like Tonykart, Birel, Topkart, CRG, Swiss Hutless, Biesse, Wright, Gillard and Kosmic spend many hundreds of thousands of pounds each year and employ many people in their quest for success. The factory drivers can earn forty to fifty thousand pounds for a season of championship kart racing. The races are supported by tyre companies such as Bridgestone, Dunlop and Vega and are seen by millions of viewers around the world. Many of these kart superstars progress through single seater car formulae to Formula 1 Grand Prix teams. Almost every current Grand Prix driver started in karts.

Formula A runs alongside Super A for its own European Championship titles, for the drivers who have newly entered these championships or have not yet attained a result sufficient for them to progress to Super A. To race in these championships a driver needs an international licence, sanctioned by both the MSA and CIK. This can be obtained by finishing in a top place in several International races, finishing in the final of a Junior European championship, or the final of the Intercontinental A (ICA) European championship. These are the routes to the top. These classes are 100cc direct drive, and race on short circuits typically of 1000 metres length. In the 125cc gearbox European Championships the lower formula is Intercontinental C (ICC), whilst the professionals race in Super ICC, the gearbox equivalent to Super A. Some of the factory drivers compete in both 100cc and 125cc gearbox.

Each continent has its own championship series, and the top finishers are then eligible for the World championships. North America is also successfully organising championships for the European style of 100cc and 125cc racing but in addition has very many classes for both two stroke and four stroke karts including the very popular laid back style for oval racing.

In Britain, the main national championships for direct drive are the Super One series for both Juniors and Seniors, and the Champions of the Future series for Juniors. Each series has a MSA British title class, Super One seniors in Formula A, Juniors in JICA (Junior Intercontinental A) and in Champions of the Future the Cadet class. These British titles are periodically tendered out by the MSA. The Association of British Kart

3

Clubs (ABkC) awards the contracts for several of the other national kart championships run by Super One. Seeded drivers finishing in the top fifteen can use their finishing place number at all member tracks.

The main gearbox classes are catered for by the Super 4 Series, again in association with the ABkC. In this case the seeded drivers are for one to nine.

Other kart classes such as the Honda Prokarts have their own Super Two national series or challenge. Very often a class will have a one-weekend open national championship, for the zero number plate. These are colloquially known as the O Plate meetings.

Race meetings are run to different levels or status. The lowest status events are Clubman, where only the club members and members of up to fifteen invited clubs may enter. These may still be large meetings at a popular club. The next is National B, where members of all clubs in an Association, such as the ABkC may be invited to enter and any number of invited clubs. National A is the status used for most national championships, where any licence holder or holder of an equivalent licence in an EU country may enter. There are very few, if any, international kart meetings in the UK, but if there were any then someone from any country with a suitable status licence recognised by the FIA could enter.

The classes and championships are covered more fully in Chapter 7.

See Chapter 7

But what exactly is a kart. The MSA definition is as follows:

"A small four wheel racing vehicle with a rigid frame and no suspension of the wheels. The engine(s) drive the rear wheels only and these wheels must be joined by a single piece rear axle with no differential action between the two rear wheels. The driver will be seated with feet forward."

Youngsters can start racing karts at the age of eight in the Cadet classes. Between age eleven and twelve they will progress to a junior class for their chosen category and by sixteen they can move into the senior classes. Juniors can start racing in an 85cc gearbox category from age 13. Only seniors can race in the 125cc, 210cc and 250cc gearbox classes and for 250cc only after seventeen years can they take part in long circuit races, gearbox racing on the traditional motor race circuits as opposed to the short circuit kart tracks otherwise used. Sixteen year olds are now permitted to race on long circuits in 125cc or 210cc classes. Novices are not permitted on long circuit, and indeed anyone starting long circuit for the first time will be required to display a novice cross. NATSKA, the schools karting association, race many classes including junior gearbox variations. There are 6,000 kart competition licence holders in the UK.

Most top racing drivers start their career in karting, but what is the typical route to the top nowadays? A kart competition licence can be gained from the tender age of eight years old. This allows these budding Formula 1 drivers to get out on a Cadet kart. There are two varieties, the 2-stroke Comer or the 4-stroke Honda, and uniquely they can race together. Top speed is around 55 mph. The Honda uses engines sealed before purchase, and with the expected long life can prove very economical. Depending on Dad's skill with the kart set-up, you would expect to see talent recognised by one or two novice trophies on the way through the first five novice licence signatures, despite the handicap of starting at the back of the grids for the heats. Next comes the daunting prospect of perhaps being on pole position for a heat. At strong clubs the Super One and Champions of the Future experts will overwhelm the relative novice but the experience will be invaluable. All the time points are being accumulated in the club championship, leading to perhaps a top six or ten finish in the first year.

If the youngster is a little older, over eleven years, he or she will probably have started in the UK's most popular class, Formula TKM with its junior variant or a restricted 125cc 2-stroke class. There is still the Honda prokart option. At thirteen there are further choices of slightly more powerful classes - JICA, Junior Rotax UK or Junior Gearbox. By the second year our future ace will be concentrating on a top three position in the club championship, and taking in one or two single-round national championships like the ABkC 'O' Plate for top grade experience. This will lead to a shot at the Super One Qualifiers held each spring. By getting into this series the karter will be up against the best in the country and gaining invaluable experience. Although it will seem a daunting task at first to even get into the A Final, the quick ones will soon be through to top ten and higher finishes.

KART LADDER

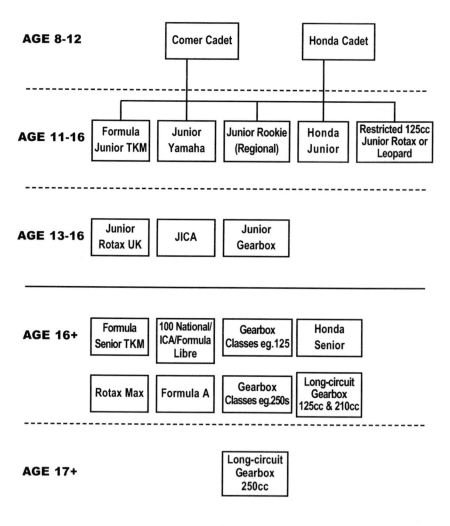

For the second year in the Super One, they should be aiming to win the title. Each year as they move up the classes, from Junior TKM to Junior Intercontinental A (JICA) and then to ICA and Formula A, the aim remains to win. By now our ace will be taking in some European competition. At this stage we are looking at costs of £20,000 to £30,000 or more per season. There is an alternative route which some take. That is to race in Italy or Belgium with one of the established European factory teams. This gets them known abroad. The next step will be for a full European and World Championship assault. The best are snapped up by works teams, several are paid salaries reputed to be up to £40,000 per annum. Getting good results here usually brings offers of single-seater test drives, some win competitions to put them on the car motorsport ladder to fame and fortune.

At 16, they can progress into cars (providing they have proved themselves in karting) and then graduate up through the single-seater classes. There is no mandatory route through the junior single-seater classes, but Formula 3 is widely considered to be an essential rung on the ladder, where young hopefuls race high-tech two-litre single seaters.

From there, the next step is Formula 3000 where they race three-litre racing cars in International competition, often at the Grand Prix meetings. For the very best young talents, Formula 3000 is the final step before Grand Prix racing, but it is a tough journey and only a very few ever make it all the way to the top.

In Britain, we enjoy a prominent position in world motor racing. Most of the Grand Prix teams are based in England, with the exception of Ferrari, Minardi, Sauber and Prost, and the great majority of the world's single-seater racing cars are built in Britain. The sheer depth of engineering expertise in this country means that motor sport earns considerable export income. More than 50,000 people are employed in the UK directly through motor sport. It is big business and Britain is the world centre for the sport.

However in karting, although there is a strong indigenous manufacturing industry, the top international teams are mainly based in Italy. Volumes for British manufacturers can be low, unless the manufacturer is also providing karts for the leisure industry. There are only two or three kart

7

engine manufacturers in the UK, Tal-ko, which makes the famous BT82 used in the ubiquitous Formula TKM classes, Apex and Solo.

Kart racing was brought to the UK by American airmen based here, in 1958, instigated by one Micky Flynn. After a successful demonstration at Silverstone in 1959 British rules were drawn up and soon large crowds were coming to meetings. For instance Shenington held an International meeting in the sixties which attracted 5,000 spectators. Art Ingels, an employee of the Kurtis Craft Company in California, built the first ever kart in 1956 and by December of the following year the Go Kart Club of America was formed.

Graham Hill was one of the first names to try karting, in 1959. Nigel Mansell cut his teeth in junior karting, then went on to dominate the 210 National gearbox class.

Reflecting the position of British kart racing is the quantity and quality of racing to be found on virtually every weekend. There are 470 race meetings in Britain at over thirty permanent race tracks. The scale of these meetings is vast; from the showcase Champions of the Future, Super Ones and Kart Grand Prix meeting to club meetings with anything from 50 to 300 plus entries depending largely on catchment area.

For many people, their first experience of karting will be as a leisure activity at their local indoor track. When well hooked, they look to expand their horizons and discover the world of competition karting. That is the time to contact a local AKRS Kart Racing School.

1.2 THE ASSOCIATION OF RACING KART SCHOOLS

At the start of the 1990s, the Association of Racing Drivers' Schools (ARDS) was formed. In the ensuing years, ARDS has become an important part of the British motor racing industry and now comprises eleven member schools operating at 15 venues. Some prominent members of ARDS and leading kart schools met with officials of the Motor Sports Association to set up a similar system for karting. A test syllabus was drawn up and the MSA agreed to recognise the inaugural ten schools with a scheme incorporating the novice driver test. A video was quickly commissioned, largely from existing material, and was replaced in 1998 with a purpose made production.

The inaugural schools set up the ARKS company to be the industry body that would set and maintain appropriate standards of tuition and operational safety. Unlike ARDS, kart clubs can apply to licence ARKS examiners to carry out the test on their behalf. Only ARKS schools though, can offer tuition under the ARKS banner with their highly-trained instructors.

The complete list of ARKS-recognised schools can be found in Chapter 8.

See Chapter 8.1

One of the major functions of the association has been, in conjunction with the MSA, to create a licensing system for school instructors and club examiners. Currently, nearly one hundred instructors and examiners have a licence. All of the instructors are required to have relevant racing experience and many of them are or have been top racing drivers.

By creating the instructor licensing system, ARKS has been able to steadily improve the standard of on-track tuition by a programme of training and development for the instructors. Not only does this benefit the customer who is assured a high-standard of professionalism, but also the individual instructor who has a qualification that is recognised throughout the industry.

In 1997, the MSA and ARKS took another important step by making the Novice Driver ARKS Test compulsory for new competition licence holders. For some time, there had been concern that novice drivers could start racing without any test of their ability or understanding of the basic rules of the sport. The now-mandatory Novice Driver ARKS Test was developed as a result and is covered in more detail in Chapter 2.1. An alternative route to gaining an MSA Competition licence is via a Kart Sport UK record card. By racing in certain promoter's series a waiver can be obtained for the driving part of the ARKS test.

See Chapter 2.1

1.3 BACK TO SCHOOL

The ARKS-recognised schools can fulfil different roles. For many of the customers who visit a school each year, it is with the intention of raising their skills to that necessary to pass the test. The schools offer training that is geared towards taking complete novices to the stage where they are ready to start their racing career. The length and content (and therefore cost!) of these courses will vary from school to school and, in several instances, can be completed by the opportunity to take part in a race using the school's equipment.

Others will go for a unique day out that allows them to experience the thrill of driving a proper kart on a race track under expert tuition. Frequently, that will be the extent of their active involvement in motorsport and all ARKS schools are geared up to provide half-day or full-day driving experience activities.

The third element of racing school business is to provide one-to-one tuition and coaching with senior instructors for those who wish to hone their newly-acquired skills.

This intensive tuition is not, however, limited to drivers in the very early stages of their careers. Often, experienced racing drivers from top championships, will call upon the services of the school instructors to help to simply go faster. As in all walks of life, the person who thinks they know it all can often be proved spectacularly wrong!

Lastly many of the schools offer a complete arrive-and-drive service for those who perhaps do not have the time or inclination to clean and maintain their own karts yet want to race, either at club level or at championship level.

Whatever your particular agenda, an ARKS-recognised school is the place to start - and perhaps continue - your active involvement in motor racing.

So what should you expect when you arrive at a racing school? Typically, the training will start with a briefing where a senior instructor will take you through the programme for the day and brief you on the essential safety aspects of the session. Suitable helmets will be provided, while trainers or racing boots that cover your ankles are needed. The school will probably have checked out your physical size and clothing requirements when you booked, to enable them to have an appropriate seat ready.

You will also sign on, something that becomes second nature before venturing onto a racing track in any capacity. There is no getting away from the fact that motor racing has an element of danger, so clubs, circuit operators and schools will all have insurance requirements. Your signing-on will in part ask you for an indemnity and be required for the operator's insurance. But don't forget that none of this will protect you against loss of earnings, so if necessary you should always have your own personal insurance.

The briefing will present you with a considerable amount of information in a fairly short space of time but it will all be relevant and important. It will include information about flag signals, how to join and leave the circuit and rules about overtaking. You will also learn how a kart works, some helpful hints on maintenance and basic set-up information. Most importantly, you will be told what to do if your kart spins or breaks down. You should raise your hand to warn other drivers and if possible drag your kart to a safe place off the track. If you are unsure about any aspect of the briefing, you should ask questions. The senior instructor will always be pleased to answer questions, either during the briefing or privately afterwards.

You will gain your first experience of the circuit in a race-ready kart. Your instructor - who will be an experienced racing driver - will use a map to show you the correct line, braking points and general circuit technique. You will most likely walk round the track with the instructor so he or she can show you all the features in more detail.

The lesson will show you how to take the corners correctly and how to brake properly. 'Slow in, fast out' is an expression you will probably hear in relation to cornering technique. Your first session will be an exploratory one, no heroics, just designed to let you learn the circuit and find out if you are comfortable.

Once onto the circuit, with the engine beside you and the wind rushing at you, it is a unique feeling. Being able to see the wheels is a novel experience along with the small steering wheel which needs only a slight movement to apply lock. However, by remembering the words of the instructor, you will get into a rhythm and each lap will come more and more naturally. Circuit driving demands intense concentration to get it right so don't be surprised if you make a mistake or two. This is quite normal, and the school will have allowed for this when planning the session.

1.4 CHOOSING A SCHOOL

The choice of where to go for tuition will be influenced by several factors, the most important one being location. The best advice is to check the list of ARKS-recognised schools in Chapter 8.1 and select the one that is most accessible for you. They all operate to the same high standards and, though each school has its own individuality, their ARKS membership is a guarantee of high standards of safety, tuition and customer-care.

Importantly, the ARKS schools all operate at circuits that have MSA circuit licences. In short, this means that the circuit you will be driving on is annually inspected by MSA officials and has met their criteria for holding race meetings or at least hold ARKS tests. You would be very unfortunate to have an accident during a school lesson, but if you did, the circuit safety facilities will meet the high standards required for race meetings.

Further, the karts used by ARKS-recognised schools will be prepared to race-ready specifications.

CHAPTER 2
SO YOU WANT TO GO RACING!

IN THIS CHAPTER

2.1 THE NOVICE DRIVER ARKS TEST
- ➤ The Starting Karting pack
- ➤ The content of the Novice Driver ARKS Test
- ➤ The examination

2.2 RACE LICENCES
- ➤ Applying for a licence
- ➤ The types of race licence
- ➤ Upgrading licences
- ➤ Licence fees

2.3 MEDICALS
- ➤ The requirement
- ➤ The test
- ➤ Medical fees

2.4 BUYING RACEWEAR
- ➤ The standards
- ➤ Crash helmets
- ➤ Overalls and other racewear
- ➤ Looking after your racewear

2.5 RACING SCHOLARSHIPS

➤ Kart scholarships

2.6 INSURANCE

➤ On and off-track insurance for karts

➤ Personal insurance

2.7 THE OFFICIALS OF THE MEETING

➤ The key officials

➤ Their responsibility and power

➤ Driver penalties

➤ The scrutineers

➤ Marshals

2.1   THE NOVICE DRIVER ARKS TEST

Once you have made the decision that you want to take your fledgling racing career a stage further, there are, of course, a number of things that you need to do. In this chapter we will take you from the beginning through to the point where you are ready to enter your very first race. This process can be completed in a matter of days, if necessary. The speed with which you progress through the various steps is entirely down to you and your particular situation.

Before anyone can go motor racing in Britain, they need to obtain a competition licence from the MSA. Although a straight-forward process, this involves several steps. The MSA will supply a Starting Karting pack which provides plenty of useful information about making a start in the sport. You can phone the MSA on 01753 765000 to get an application form for the pack. They now take credit cards or you need to send a cheque for £31.00. You will also be able to purchase the Starting Karting pack from an ARKS School, so you might save the postage. In the pack will be the kart race licence application form and a list of ARKS-recognised schools and club examiners details. Then, if over 18, a medical examination is required to ensure that the candidate is fit enough to go racing. You can start racing from age 8, and from that age to 17, no medical is required, just a self-declaration of fitness. From 18, the initial medical is all that is required, thereafter self-certification applies until the age of 45. After that age a medical is required each year.

See Chapter 2.2 & 2.3

Unless you are already experienced in driving a racing class of kart outdoors you will definitely need some training and acclimatisation before entering for the test. An ARKS school is the best place for that training, although if you already have your own kart you may wish to take it to a circuit that permits private practice and acclimatise on your own. However there is a danger of starting bad habits which could be difficult to eradicate later. Many of the ARKS schools will be happy to train you on your own kart. Then, when ready, arrange with an ARKS school or Club Examiner for your ARKS Test. During this test, the candidate will be instructed in basic racing skills and complete a written test to check their understanding of essential safety regulations, flag signals and basic kart control. There are some exemptions to the need to take the test. These are:

- Anyone who held a Restricted or National B Kart Licence at any time during 1999, 2000 or 2001.

- Anyone who can provide proof of having ever held a Kart or Race Licence of higher status than National B.

- Anyone who can provide proof of holding a National Schools Karting Association (Nat SKA) National licence during 2000, 2001 or 2002.

- Anyone who, being a foreign national, can produce proof from their ASN (country motorsport association) that they have the necessary karting experience.

It is still recommended that the Starting Karting pack be purchased to achieve familiarisation with the kart racing regulations.

A race National B licence or higher grade also entitles the holder to enter Kart Clubman or National B status events, but not higher. In this case the holder will still be classified as a novice until six signatures have been gathered at six kart meetings. The ARKS test counts as one of the signatures.

When you attend for the ARKS Test you will need to take the kart race licence application form with the medical certificate section already completed. You must have filled in your name and personal details before you attend for your medical (if you are over 18). And, don't forget that if you are under 18, you must have parental approval. You will need to pay for the test, currently £56. You need to make out a cheque for that amount to ARKS (if with a Club Examiner) or the school (where VAT may be added). If you are also hiring a kart or other equipment from the school to do the test in, there will be an extra charge. Club Examiners cannot hire equipment to you, so this route is only applicable if you have your own kart and equipment. But each Club Examiner is linked to a school so hires may be possible via their school.

During the ARKS test, you will be shown the video that comes as part of the Starting Karting pack. It covers all the points you need to know to pass the test and it is worth watching the video several times before going for the test. The video runs for around 15 to 20 minutes and covers a host of information that will be useful during the test and as you make a start in the sport. Your instructor will emphasise some of the points made in the video, and will welcome any questions about it. You will almost certainly walk round the track with the instructor to learn the entry and exit points, and the racing line for each corner. This might be undertaken or reinforced using a diagram in the classroom.

You will then take to the track in a recognised class of kart for your first session of acclimatisation. Your driving will be assessed with the emphasis on correct technique and application of the classroom teaching and the lessons learnt from the video and the guidance notes contained in the pack. After feedback from your instructor you may be able to have one more session on the track, otherwise you will return to the track for the observed test session.

After the on-track session (or it could be before), you have to take a written exam. To pass the test, you must score at least 66% in the first part of the driving assessment and 100% in the second part, along with 80% in the written assessment. However, passing the test alone is not necessarily enough as approval from the senior instructor is still required. This requirement places a responsibility on the ARKS school and the senior instructor to satisfy themselves that the candidate is fit to race and has sufficient understanding of the rules of the sport. It is in the best interests of the candidate and existing racers that this decision is not taken lightly, as an irresponsible or ill-equipped driver is a potential hazard to fellow racers. If you only pass one section, you will be able to get a pass certificate for that, and not be required to take that part again.

There is nothing complex or tricky about the ARKS Test, but you will need to show a reasonable understanding of the basic rules of the sport to be successful. An important element of the test is to check the candidates' knowledge of the flag signals used throughout the sport. If you should fail the assessment, the test can be re-taken and you should discuss this with the school on the day of the test.

Remember that, if after watching the video at home, you feel that you may not be properly prepared to take the test, make contact with the ARKS school where you intend to go for the test. If you express your concerns to the school, they should be able to provide some on-track tuition and coaching to help you prepare for the test. By doing this, you will increase the chance of passing the test at the first attempt.

2.2 RACE LICENCES

The full rules and regulations concerning competition licences are contained within the current edition of the MSA Competitors Yearbook (known as the 'Blue Book'). This publication should be consulted at all times.

When you have successfully completed the ARKS test you can apply to the MSA for your first kart race licence. The application form should be sent, along with the appropriate fee, to the MSA and it will normally take one to two weeks for the application to be processed and the licence returned. An express system is available at an additional fee for those drivers who need their licence within three working days. There is a system whereupon, if you have been exempted from the medical because of your age, you can take your application form with the ARKS Test pass stamped on it, to your first race meeting along with the fee, and the MSA Steward will accept it in lieu of a licence. The Competition Secretary will then send it on to the MSA on your behalf, and the licence will be sent to you in due course. This means you could take your test the day before your first race. If you do this, be sure to obtain a note from the MSA Steward to confirm that you raced in a satisfactory manner, because your licence will not be available for a signature.

RACING LICENCES

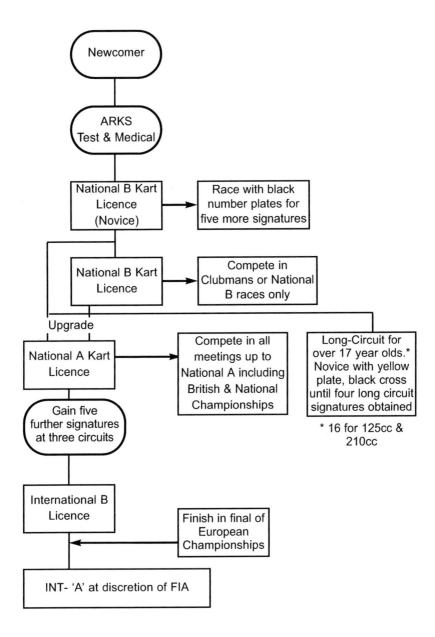

All competition licences are valid until the end of the current year and so if you are granted a licence in the middle of the season, you will still need to renew it on January 1st for the following year.

There are two levels of National race licence, known as National A and National B. When you have passed the medical examination or completed the self-certification and passed your ARKS Test, you can apply for a National B licence. You must also join an MSA-recognised kart club, and if you intend to enter any of the ABkC National championships you should ensure your chosen club is a member of this association. Holding the licence and club card will qualify you to race at any club in the UK that has invited your club or association. Remember that not all categories of racing are open to holders of National B licences. Typically, some of the championship meetings are only open to holders of a higher-grade licence, and may also require pre-qualification. Also some classes are only open to certain age groups. For instance, to race at long circuit meetings in 250cc you must be over 17 and not be a novice.

Anyone starting racing under a National B licence must use black number plates on the kart until they have satisfactorily completed five more races. The ARKS Test gives the first signature of the total of six required. During this time you will have to start at the back of the grids in the heats, along with other novices, but can qualify for the position you earn in the heats for the grid for the final. If there is timed qualifying then the start from the back rule does not apply.

The MSA Steward will observe the racing and if he or she is satisfied that the driver has performed satisfactorily and finished the race without undue incident he will sign the reverse of the licence. Normally the Steward will not sign the licence unless the driver has achieved a finish for at least 50% of the races they have competed in.

To qualify for a licence signature, the driver needs to present his licence to the race officials when signing-on at the start of the meeting.

See Chapter 4.3

If the driver has performed satisfactorily, he will then be able to collect his licence at the end of the meeting with another signature on the reverse. However, don't forget that there is a statutory 30-minute period after the provisional race results are published during which competitors have the right to protest the results. Licences may not be released until that 30-minute period has ended.

When the signatures are all collected the driver has the choice of continuing with the National B licence or upgrading to a National A licence. There is an upgrading fee, and so if only club meetings are to be entered then a National B may suffice. However you will need to keep the licence or licences safe and be prepared to show the signatures to prove you are no longer a novice. If a driver then has ambitions to progress into international events, a similar up-grading process is necessary to move from a National A licence to an International B licence. The requirement is for signatures from five National B or A level events at a minimum of three different venues. For those competing at the very highest level of the sport there is one further grade of International licence, only issued with the authority of the FIA regulations. Remember to get your licence signed, you never know when you might need the evidence.

So for most drivers wishing to compete in Britain, a National A licence is sufficient. It is also worth noting that the higher-grade licences attract a much higher annual fee and have more stringent medical examination requirements!

The relevant 2002 licence fees are as follows:

National B	**£21**
National A	**£32**
International B	**£83**
International A	**£89**

It cannot be stressed too much just how important your race licence is. If you fail to produce your licence when signing-on for a race meeting, you face a fine or exclusion from the meeting. Further, all licences must be signed by the holder and have a passport size photograph of the holder permanently attached. Failure to have a photograph properly attached may lead to the licence being rejected by race officials.

Consider trying to find a passport photo booth close to Rowrah on a wet Sunday morning in March..... If you are going to go racing, you need to keep the paperwork in order!

In just the same way that you can have your road licence endorsed or withdrawn, so can penalties be applied to your competition licence. If your on-track (and, indeed, off-track) conduct is considered inappropriate, your licence can be endorsed or withdrawn by the power of the officials of the meeting.

Breaches of the rules and regulations whilst competing can be punished by endorsement and three such driving penalties will lead to a ban from racing for a period of time that can range from 30 days to many years. It should also be remembered that your conduct out of the kart and indeed that of members of your team can also come under scrutiny.

One sure-fire way of losing your racing licence is to follow up an on-track incident with a physical confrontation in the paddock after the race. A number of drivers have lost their licences for such incidents. In some cases, they have been banned from racing for five years.

Your licence will also be marked if your kart fails technical scrutineering. This sort of record should not count towards driving disqualification but the Steward will still take the licence from you at the end of the meeting after a total of three signatures, for the MSA's consideration of the offences. There is an appeal system, but it rarely works in your favour for driving or conduct offences except in the most extenuating of circumstances.

Although it is no longer necessary to notify the MSA if you are disqualified from driving on the public highway, the MSA retains the right to act against a driver who loses their road traffic licence in a manner which is deemed to bring motorsport into disrepute.

2.3 MEDICALS

The full rules and regulations concerning medicals are contained within the current edition of the MSA Competitors Yearbook (known as the 'Blue Book'. This publication should be consulted at all times.)

ARE YOU SURE YOU WANT TO BE A RACING DRIVER?

FOLEY

MEDICALS

All first-time applicants for kart race licences over the age of 18 must pass a medical examination by their doctor before applying for their licence. After the first year, they will not then need a medical examination until the age of 45, although a medical self-declaration is required annually. International licence holders must, however, pass a medical examination each year. A fee (usually at least £50) will normally be charged by the doctor for the examination and must be paid directly to the doctor at the time.

The medical is similar to that which is carried out for life assurance assessment, but with specific attention to conditions such as diabetes, epilepsy and heart conditions. In such cases, a separate examination and review by the MSA Medical Consultant may be required. Eyesight is also checked and, of course, glasses or contact lenses are permitted, although if used to pass the test, they must then be used when racing.

It is now possible for disabled drivers to obtain a kart race licence although each case is considered on merit. Any potential applicant should contact the British Motor Sports Association for the Disabled in the first instance for specific advice. The MSA can give details.

See Chapter 8.3

2.4 BUYING RACEWEAR

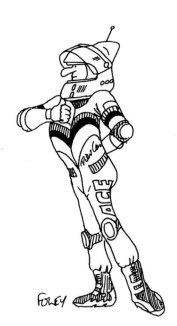

BUYING RACEWEAR

The full rules and regulations concerning race wear are contained within the current edition of the MSA Competitors Yearbook (known as the 'Blue Book'). This publication should be consulted at all times.

The next step on the journey towards your first race is to buy the mandatory clothing and crash helmet. The MSA publishes information in the Blue Book about the standard of equipment required and the minimum for clothing is an approved kart race suit.

The racesuit must either be approved by the CIK or FMK (predecessor to the CIK) or the MSA, or be of leather. If the former it will have a label sewn in to show the FMK or CIK or MSA registration number.

Only leather suits or those specifically approved by the MSA are permitted for long circuit racing. They shall be a minimum of 1.2mm thickness. They may be of two piece construction so long as they are zipped together. Unlike motor racing where overalls are fireproof, in karting it is the abrasion proof and strength which is important. Sometimes prokart four-stroke endurance racing can obtain a waiver for the drivers to permit motor race overalls. It is important to ensure that the racesuit complies with the appropriate standard as this will be checked by the scrutineers before the start of the meeting and you will not be permitted to use racesuits that do not comply.

If you are buying a kartsuit for the first time, there is a wide range of styles and standards to suit all pockets. The cheapest overalls that meet the relevant standard can be bought for around £100. However, if you can afford a more expensive suit it will be a good investment. Many of the racesuit manufacturers will make to measure for a small extra charge. The best advice is to buy from a well-known outlet and seek advice from knowledgeable staff about what is best for you. Never practice or race without wearing the correct type of kart suit. Racesuits to the current specification will usually be made with a material called 'Cordura©'. Older style polycotton suits with a CIK three figure number will be phased out by the end of 2004.

Drivers must also wear strong gloves and boots that give ankle protection and do not have any holes in the soles. Specially manufactured racing boots are a good investment. On a practical note, racesuits and boots will last longer if treated with care. If you work on your own kart at race meetings, and most people do, it is always worth changing out of your racesuit or at least wearing a mechanic's apron. If the wife/partner/lover is kind, they may also offer to wash your racesuit from time to time. Take special care to follow the instructions as they are made of rather different materials.

In wet weather most people use a wetsuit to cover and protect their racesuit. It is also a good idea to slip an outer boot over the racing boots when walking around before and after the race. All clothing and helmets that are intended to be used, including your second-best wet weather racesuit and gloves must be presented for scrutineering before use.

Crash helmets must also meet the standard specified by the MSA and, once more, it is wise to buy the best crash helmet that your budget will stretch to. Along with your racesuit, your crash helmet must be presented to the scrutineers when the kart is checked before the meeting and they will be checking for obvious signs of damage as well as the required approval stickers.

The fit of a crash helmet is critical and it should be neither too tight nor too loose. A helmet should be as closely-fitting as possible whilst still being comfortable. Take specialist advice when buying a helmet and take time to find the right size for you. For International events the helmet must weigh less than 1400gms for Juniors or 1800gms for Seniors. Younger drivers will need the smallest shell sizes made and special checks should be made for a correct fit. Do not be surprised if the scrutineer asks to have the younger driver put on their helmet for a check. Contrary to what is often said of racing drivers, the head is valuable and it is worth protecting it. If you are unlucky enough to have an accident and bang your head, don't be surprised if the officials confiscate your crash helmet. It will certainly have the MSA approval sticker removed if there is any doubt, and it may also be sent with you in the ambulance so the doctors can see any damage.

Though there may be no obvious external signs of damage, modern crash helmets are designed so that, in the case of a severe blow, the helmet will partially absorb the impact. In such a case, the event scrutineers are empowered to impound any helmet they consider no longer safe for use. If this happens, rather than feel aggrieved at the cost of replacing your helmet, feel thankful that it did the job it was designed to do. Crash helmets are only impounded for the safety of the driver concerned.

For your own safety, look after your crash helmet. If you ever drop it, you must, at the very least, return it to the manufacturer for proper inspection. Damage may not be readily apparent.

Currently, the acceptable helmet standards are:

BS 6658 - 85 "A" and "A/FR" (Type "B" is not acceptable). (Helmets over ten years old may not be acceptable in future).

Snell SA95 (acceptable until 31.12.05).
SFI Foundation 31.1, 31.2 (two years of UK use anticipated). Not permitted for International competition.
Snell SA2000 (the latest standard with at least 10 years life anticipated). The European E22 standard is NOT permitted.

Helmets must also carry a fluorescent blue MSA approval sticker. Check this with the supplier before making your purchase. These standards are regularly reviewed and updated and older standards may become no longer acceptable. If your helmet goes out of date there is no choice but to buy a new one. Higher grades of scrutineers or certain MSA headquarters staff are empowered to check and affix the sticker for a small fee. You must have the MSA sticker before racing and it will be checked at scrutineering.

A soft bag to carry your helmet in is a good idea, as this will help keep it clean and free from scratches. Some people even retain the box that the helmet came in when new as a useful place to store it safely. Your crash helmet will be a major element of your initial spend so it is important to look after it properly. Only clean it with soap and water and read the manufacturer's instructions before putting any stickers on it.

You will see some wonderful helmet designs, particularly in Grand Prix racing. However, don't try and do something yourself, as some types of paint or stickers could be harmful to the helmet. If you want a smart design or your sponsors colours on your helmet, go to one of the specialist helmet painters who will know exactly what to do and, importantly, what not to do! Make sure you do not remove or paint over the helmet standard sticker, keep it well protected.

2.5 RACING SCHOLARSHIPS

Occasionally there may be a scholarship or prize-drive offered in a championship. It is rare for these to pay for all racing costs but still may be worthwhile because of the exposure obtained. Beware of certain traders offering sponsored drives. Use of a poor chassis for a year could spoil that season completely. On the other hand once you have achieved

RACING SCHOLARSHIPS

a good reputation a trader may offer you a free loan of equipment. Often you will have to help in the team or coach junior drivers in return. Sometimes kart drivers are invited to test a racing car through a sponsor's affiliation. Any opportunity like this should be worthwhile, but remember your fellow invitees may be secretly testing a car to help with their prowess in the test.

2.6 INSURANCE

Just like anything in life, you can insure your kart as well as ancillary equipment like trailers, tools, spares and garage equipment. One or two insurers might even insure your kart whilst it is being raced, but more usually the insurance covers everything but racing. Often there are strict conditions about how it is secured overnight at the paddock - an awning is hardly a secure area. Usually the premium is set by the value of the equipment taking into account any previous history of claims you have made. The MSA's insurers have a scheme to insure racing vehicles, as do many other insurance companies and specialist brokers. Check out the ads in the karting magazines.

If most drivers worked out the value of tools and spares they have stashed away in their garage, they would probably be very surprised.

Finally, the drivers themselves really ought to be properly insured. Of course, you may be covered through other existing policies but before starting racing it is advisable to inform current insurers that you are participating in motor sport. The majority of life insurance companies will exclude motorsport unless it was accepted at the outset, but it is well worth checking as different companies exclude different levels of motorsport. If they do accept motorsport, seek that confirmation in writing!

Once again, there is no requirement to have any insurance cover and a small amount is automatically provided to all competition licence holders. It is important at this stage to take proper advice about your liabilities and then arrange cover accordingly. If your existing policies exclude motor racing, it is quite easy to arrange a specific or top up policy through one of the specialist motor sport insurers.

This is often a badly-neglected area but is worthy of very careful consideration. For instance, a married man in his 40s with a wife, two children and a mortgage, should be looking for £500,000 or more in life cover. Obviously, a 17 year-old with no dependants may not need anything like as much cover, but the cost of living with permanent injury following a serious accident should not be discounted. Packages can be tailored to suit individual needs and further investigation is strongly encouraged.

If you race abroad it is even more essential to have insurance. Your holiday travel policy will be unlikely to cover competition driving, so seek specialist advice before leaving. Medical costs in most countries are very high.

Two other areas of insurance should also be covered. If you are racing or testing on a licensed track or training with an ARKS-recognised school, public liability cover should be automatically provided by the organisers of that activity. However, if you make private arrangements to test your kart at a local airfield for instance, you will have no such cover. Finally, if your racing team grows in size and becomes more professional, it may be worth considering a small business policy.

2.7 THE OFFICIALS OF THE MEETING

Contrary to what some drivers may feel at times, the officials of the meeting are there to ensure the meeting runs smoothly, safely and in accordance to the relevant rules and regulations. They are not simply there to make life difficult for drivers!

Before we go any further on this subject, there is something very important to be said, something that most drivers seem to forget at some point. Virtually every official in motor racing you will come into contact with is a volunteer giving up his or her time so that you can race. At best, they will be receiving modest expenses. They love the sport as much as you do, perhaps more.

Starting from the top is the headmaster for the day, the Clerk of the Course. He is top dog and if you are called to see him, it is unlikely

THE RACING OFFICIALS

that he wishes to congratulate you on a particularly fine piece of driving! The CoC is responsible for the overall safe conduct of the meeting and is usually the first point of call for drivers who have committed some misdemeanour.

By the very nature of the job, the CoC carries considerable authority and is often called upon to make tough decisions on a whole raft of subjects, including imposing penalties on drivers, when to stop races, track and weather conditions and many more. It is probable that, if called to see the CoC after qualifying or a race, he will be acting upon a report received from one of his observers or Assistant Clerks.

These senior marshals or assistant Clerks of the Course are stationed around the track, and will be reporting back to race control (the nerve centre of the race meeting) about what drivers are getting up to. Be warned: Clerks of the Course have heard just about every excuse in the

OFFICIALS AT A RACE MEETING

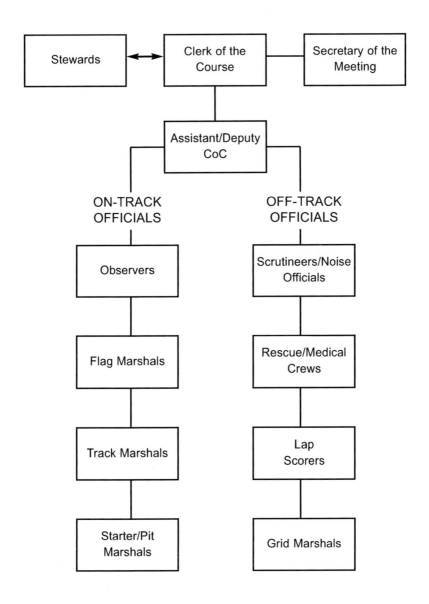

book before, so if you are guilty of a misdemeanour, you're better off taking it on the chin!

The CoC is also the judicial body dealing with any protests raised by competitors. He has the power to penalise or exclude drivers and impose fines.

Should a driver appeal against any such penalty, this will then be heard by the Stewards of the Meeting. At race meetings there will be three Stewards, one of them appointed by the MSA and two by the club. The MSA Steward will have taken novice licences and those presented for upgrading and will thus be observing your driving. The Stewards have no involvement in the running of the meeting and are the second judicial body at a race meeting. They will hear and adjudicate on any appeal against a decision of the CoC. The Stewards will also report on the running of the meeting to the MSA.

Working closely with the CoC is the Secretary of the Meeting, who will often be the first point of contact for competitors. The Secretary will handle the administration of the meeting, including receiving entries, organising competitors signing-on and looking after a hundred and one other things. The Secretary will often double up as the Chief Results official as well.

All competitors will come into contact with the event scrutineers, who fall into two distinct categories. Before the start of practice, competitors are required to present their karts for scrutineering when the basic safety of the vehicle will be checked along with the drivers' helmet, overalls, boots and gloves.

See Chapter 4.3

Some race meetings, particularly of a higher status, will also have eligibility scrutineers on duty. Typically, these officials will be appointed to specific championships or classes to check the compliance with the rules of the competing karts. They have the power to measure components, oversee the stripping of engines or components and apply and remove seals on controlled items. Often, the eligibility scrutineer will examine successful karts in detail at the end of the race to check compliance with the rules. An alternative employed is to seal the engine or component until it can be made available to the eligibility scrutineer at a later date. Fuel samples may be taken and put in sealed containers for laboratory analysis. Results will be provisional until the results of such tests are known.

Working in conjunction with the scrutineers, and becoming ever-more important, is the environmental scrutineer. This is the man with the noise meter and, with new noise regulations coming into effect from January 1999 and even more stringent limits from 2001, his role is crucial. The noise levels generated by competing karts will be checked at any time on the racetrack. If your kart exceeds the limit, it is your responsibility to sort it out and reduce the noise to an acceptable level. Do not rant and rave at the scrutineers, they are protecting the future of the sport.

The need to make the sport as environmentally friendly as possible is a pressing issue and noise testing is becoming more vigorous each year. There have been several instances of race leaders being black-flagged (called into the pits) due to their karts recording excessive readings on noise meters. The silencing system on a kart must be carefully prepared and maintained in good condition.

Out on the track, aside from the observers, are teams of flag marshals and incident marshals. The flag marshals are there to communicate information to the drivers via a range of coloured flags. The colours of the flags and their meanings will have been covered in preparation for the ARKS Test. Drivers who fail to respond to these flags put themselves and their fellow racers in danger and, at the least, could find themselves up before the CoC with some serious explaining to do!

See Chapter 8.5

The incident marshals are the people you least want to come into contact with. That's not because they aren't nice people... They will be the guys (and girls) who descend upon you should you be unlucky enough to fall off. You may be upset at having just parked the results of months of labour in the tyre wall, but it wasn't their fault, so don't take out your frustrations on them. Their priorities are to deal with any fires (thankfully very rare) and then get you to a position of safety and your kart as far out of harm's way as possible. If you are uninjured though, you should pull your kart to a place of safety as quickly as possible.

Also, should your pride and joy fail to last the distance, the incident marshals will direct you to a place of safety. Follow their instructions! Here, a word of warning. You may think you can coax an ailing kart back to the pits but if you are caught on the racing line when the battling leaders come over the brow, you could have serious problems.

Far better, if the kart is failing, to pull off in good time where you can guide the kart well clear of the track and into a position of safety at the direction of the marshals. Too often, karts have drifted to a halt in a position that puts the driver in danger, the marshals in danger having to move it and the other drivers in danger as they dodge around it. If in doubt, park it sooner rather than later.

Consider the fact that previously undamaged karts left in foolish positions have, moments later, been written off by an out-of-control rival.

There are many other race officials who perform vital but often unseen roles. The lapscorers, timekeepers, medical and rescue staff, pit, paddock and startline marshals are all there working away behind the scenes. In all dealings with officials, be courteous and professional and you shouldn't go far wrong! If you want to know more about marshalling, contact the British Motor Racing Marshals' Club.

See Chapter 8.3

Chapter 3
So now you have a licence

IN THIS CHAPTER

3.1 CHOOSING A CATEGORY

➤ Kart clubs

➤ The diversity of British karting

➤ What does it all cost?

➤ How to choose a category

3.2 D-I-Y OR PROFESSIONAL TEAM?

➤ Buying or hiring a kart

➤ The likely costs

➤ Professional teams

➤ Where to find a kart

3.3 BUYING A KART

➤ Making the right choice

➤ Negotiating to buy a kart

➤ What to look out for

3.4 KART PREPARATION

➤ Making it safe and legal

➤ Checking the basics

➤ Checking the engine

3.5 TESTING

- ➤ The importance of testing
- ➤ When and where to test
- ➤ Planning the test day
- ➤ Setting targets

3.6 MENTAL AND PHYSICAL PREPARATION FOR THE DRIVER

- ➤ The physical and mental challenge
- ➤ In the office
- ➤ Food and drink before the event and on race day
- ➤ Personal fitness

3.7 DRIVER COACHING

- ➤ The benefits of coaching
- ➤ The ARKS-instructor as a coach

3.1 Choosing a category

Around 30 kart clubs organise racing in the UK. Some have leases on circuits but most have to hire the track for their races from the circuit owners. Each club must be organised democratically and, via an annual general meeting, elect a committee and chairman to administer the club. The club committee will set the fees such as annual membership and entry fees. Some clubs offer race entry fee discounts to club members. Usually there will be an annual dinner dance where the club championship trophies are presented. Get to know the chairman, secretary, competition secretary and committee. They will value your comments and might encourage you to offer yourself for election to the committee.

Most kart clubs organise one club meeting per month, sometimes missing out the winter months. This is usually on the same weekend each month, so that drivers can plan to regularly race at one, two or more meetings per month at different circuits. Often challenge series will visit the club meetings as part of their championship. In between the club meetings there might well be special championship series meetings.

You must be a member of a kart club to go racing. You may choose to join more than one, perhaps to gain points in other club championships, or benefit from the membership discounts. It is a good idea to try and do as many meetings as possible at your local club. That way you will be getting points in their club championship and perhaps a good overall position, maybe even a trophy. This will earn recognition from your peers in the class you have chosen.

But do take the chance to race at different circuits. If you plan to enter a national championship series the following year, look and see which circuits they normally visit. Then try and visit each for a club race to learn the circuits. This will stand you in good stead.

Some clubs specialise in different aspects of racing, for instance four-stroke classes. Find out which classes are popular at your local clubs and join one that suits you and your chosen kart. It is not much fun racing if there are only two or three karts in your class. Nearly all clubs will cater for the ubiquitous Formula TKM classes and the newer Rotax Max class.

On the other hand some may not run gearbox classes at all, either through choice or track restrictions. Some may not run four-stroke classes, others may run nothing but.

See Chapter 7

Kart categories can be broadly split into three groups. Direct drive two-stroke, known historically as Class 1, gearbox classes known as Class 4 and four-stroke categories, initially derived from the leisure industry but with more purpose built engines appearing. Endurance racing usually uses four-strokes, so several people can share the driving, pit work and, of course, the costs. Endurance series may also be organised for the Rotax Max class.

So just how much does it all cost? There is no simple answer to this question. However, it is certainly true to say that it does not need to cost as much as many people first think.

At the top level, the sport is certainly not cheap, but can offer higher power-to-weight ratios and more racing than most affordable car racing categories. You would not be able to contest a season of Formula A championship racing in this country for less than £15,000, and it would be twice that with a top team. Race in the European and World championships as well and your budget would soon escalate to beyond £50,000.

However, these budgets only apply to a very small number of the 6000 people who go kart racing in Britain each year, many of whom race competitively on very limited resources. If you have £2,000 to spend over the year, you can most certainly get started in karting, less in some classes.

Before you reach the grid for your first race, there are several areas of expenditure that cannot be avoided. Earlier we mentioned the steps towards gaining a competition licence. These will cost around £220 in the first year (£170 if you do not need a medical) but will be less than £70 in subsequent seasons. This includes membership of a kart club.

The choice of which category to enter is one of the most difficult decisions to make. The best way of making the correct choice is to spend some time researching the classes available. A few Sundays spent at kart meetings will be a good investment. By watching the different classes and visiting the paddock, you will get a good feel for what each class is about.

You will find most kart drivers very approachable and their comments will give pointers to which class is right for you. Local traders and kart schools are other valuable sources of information. By taking some time to get a feel for the sport before making a choice, prospective karters can save themselves making the wrong decision. Buy the kart magazines and read about the different classes.

See Chapter 3.3

3.2 D-I-Y OR PROFESSIONAL TEAM?

Once you have made your choice of category, there is another important decision to be made. Do you prepare and maintain your own kart, or do you have this work done professionally? This decision will really depend upon your resources, in terms of time, money and technical ability.

You will be able to do most of the work on a kart yourself, with one exception. Engine re-builds are best left to the experts. Karts are relatively uncomplicated, the art is in setting them up to suit the track. So if you have a reasonable mechanical understanding, or have friends with that ability, it is relatively easy to run a kart yourself. The great majority of kart racers maintain and run their own karts, or those of their sons and daughters.

If you don't have too much money, concentrate on getting a good kart and running it yourself. You will probably be surprised at how low the cost of going racing can be. It really does not need to cost telephone number budgets. If you do run the kart yourself, you will learn a great deal about setting up a competition vehicle.

For instance, you could buy a respectable Formula TKM or prokart for £1200 and, barring accident damage or major engine failures, spend the same again contesting a season of 12 meetings if you run the kart yourself. It may sound obvious, but it is important to discipline yourself not to crash! If you are going out trying to win races and are crashing all the time, you will never make any progress.

However, if you are short on mechanical knowledge or time, you may need to use a professional team. You then have two choices. You can buy the kart and engines and have the team maintain them and bring them to the meetings for you, supplying a mechanic to help you race. Alternatively the team could hire you all the racing equipment you will need. You simply arrive at the circuit and drive the kart. The cost of this work depends partly on your racing category and partly how far you and team need to travel to the race meetings.

You could expect a team to charge at least £200 per day to bring your own kart, supply a mechanic, and run you out of their awning. This would rise to £400 or more if you used the team's kart. Travel and accommodation costs would be on top if far from base. In 100cc championship classes even top drivers often hire their engines from a reputable engine tuner. That way they are guaranteed fresh engines for each round and do not have to bear directly the initial cost of the engine and tuning, or take the risk of the depreciation at the end of the season. Depending on the deal you have with a team, you will normally have to pay for all the consumables, engine rebuilds, tyres, entry fees and of course accident damage.

Many of the ARKS Kart Schools run their own race teams and would be pleased to discuss budgets or kart hire.

At least one insurance company will cover karts whilst racing but most policies merely cover the equipment at all times except when racing. With a kart, the cost of accident damage is not usually too high.

See Chapter 2.6

By far the most popular route for karters is to buy their own kart and prepare and maintain it themselves in their spare time. Often, friends and family become involved, both before the races and during the event by acting as pit crew, pushers and helpers.

Second-hand karts can be bought for under £1500. If the kart is then maintained to a good standard, it will lose little of its value during the season. New karts in economy classes start at less than £2,000, and go on up to say £8,000 for a 250cc gearbox kart with all the bodywork. So yet again, it much depends on which category you choose.

The best place to find details of karts for sale is in the classified pages of the monthly kart magazine, Karting Magazine. This is essential reading for prospective racers and a vital source of karts and equipment. And if you do well in the races, you will be able to read about yourself! But another good source of second-hand karts are adverts in the paddock or race control building, especially in the autumn after the main championships are over. Do not forget your local trader either, he will often have a stock of trade-ins. Internet sites such as www.karting.co.uk have a thriving sales page.

Just as you would when buying a second-hand car, check the credentials of the seller. Beware if chassis or engine numbers appear to have been altered. Alarm bells will ring if the price seems exceptionally low. Karting magazines and the internet often carry lists of stolen equipment.

If you are running the kart yourself you will need a means of getting the kart to the circuit. Maybe it will go in the back of an estate car, with the wheels and pods removed. Or even on a roof-rack, with the engine removed to keep the weight down. Small trailers are favoured, either open or the van type where you could have a workbench and hang an awning outside for the kart. Their advantage is in being able to leave the trailer in the paddock whilst you go off in your car to seek an evening meal or bed and breakfast. Many karters stay on the circuit, in a caravan or motorhome, and there is a great atmosphere amongst the teams in the evening preceding race-day. If your budget stretches to a van, it can perhaps double up as sleeping accommodation.

There really is a category to suit every pocket. It is far better to start off in a relatively lowly class and work your way up as you learn, rather than come in at too high a level and end up broke and disillusioned.

3.3 BUYING A KART

Kart preparation really starts before you've even bought the kart. The best advice is to go to a number of race meetings and start having a look around at the sort of categories that appeal to you. Then, when you've identified the type of category you want to race in and sorted out how much money you can afford to spend, go and talk to as many competitors in that class as possible.

This will give you background information about the various karts and will help you build up a picture about which are the most popular karts for the class you have chosen. But always bear in mind that some views may be biased! Often you will find different models of kart are more popular at one track than another. This is often because of support from a local trader. A good local trader will be invaluable if you suddenly need a spare part to fix your kart. This might influence your choice of kart.

On the other hand, some makes of chassis might go better at one track rather than another. Some chassis might go better in the winter, when it is cold and wet, rather than in the summer when it is hot. In the end it is the nut behind the wheel that makes the biggest difference to winning, crashing or coming last.

When you are at race meetings looking at the options, take time to go and speak to the event scrutineers. Go to the meeting early and watch the pre-race scrutineering going on. This will give you useful pointers as to what the officials are looking for when they make the mandatory safety checks on each kart. During the middle of the day when there is not a queue of karts waiting to be checked, seek out one of the scrutineers and tell them of your plans.

They will normally be happy to share some of their knowledge about what to look out for from a safety and scrutineering point of view when buying a kart. Although they rightly carry considerable powers during a race meeting, scrutineers are enthusiasts who volunteer their time and effort for little reward. Providing you pick a sensible time to approach them and explain your situation, you should gain benefit from their knowledge.

When you do start negotiating to buy a kart, talk to the seller about how much help they can provide initially when you purchase it. Quite often, if someone is selling a kart they are either giving up racing completely, moving to another category or buying a new chassis for the following season. In most cases, they will want to give you all the information you need about running the kart. In motorsport, everyone who takes part is enthusiastic about the sport, so try and use that enthusiasm to your advantage!

There is a lot of free advice out there and before anybody puts their money down on a kart, they must try to contain their enthusiasm. Most people can't wait to get started and rush out and buy a kart, without knowing what it's all about. Then they waste the first few months

resolving problems that could have been avoided with proper research and a degree of patience! The best advice is; don't rush in.

The more ground work you do, the more successful you will be and the more fun you will have when you first start. Make sure you take a look at a number of karts before making any decision. This will help you build up knowledge of the market and ensure that you ultimately make a good choice. It is invariably a buyer's market, so use that to your advantage.

When you decide how much to spend on a kart, make sure you leave enough room in your budget to actually be able to run the kart in races. Even the basics like fuel, tyres and entry fees need to be paid for out of your precious reserves.

The regulations for the different classes that are run on a national basis are all contained in the 2002 Kart Race Yearbook, known as the 'Gold Book', issued by the MSA. Associations such as the ABkC have adopted or adapted certain classes in line with the demands of drivers, and any such variations will be shown in that booklet. Sometimes a new class springs up, usually at the behest of a trader or manufacturer, and may be authorised by the MSA. To begin with it may only race at one or two tracks, so be cautious in buying such equipment. If in doubt, check with the MSA and seek a copy of the regulations.

When you first start there is not usually a need to buy a kart with a winning pedigree. But if you are moving from another racing category, say motocross, and think you will quickly be on the pace, you might well want to start with a race-proven winner. Just be a little careful. Most kart folk are pretty honest, but it might be a good idea to note the engine and chassis numbers during the race day. Some people have sold the same winning engine six times over, for a much enhanced price. So if you are going to buy such a kart or engine, where its price will almost certainly be enhanced by its pedigree, try and arrange to take it away at the end of its last race with its current owner. Too often, a winning kart has returned to its base before collection by the proud new purchaser and lost some of the best bits and pieces in the process!

If the seller is giving up karting, then you could expect a package to include many of the other essentials, such as a trolley, spare wheels, wet weather tyres, maybe even a trailer. Such a package is very worthwhile. Even if they are changing categories you could expect a set of wet weather tyres and perhaps some spare slicks on wheels or just some spare tyres.

The first thing to look at when inspecting a kart is how clean is it? That will actually be a good indication of how well prepared the kart is. If the kart is filthy and has got dirt and grease all over it, then the odds are that the standard of preparation will be quite poor. If a kart is really clean and well presented, as racing karts should always be, then you at least know that the owner has been paying some attention to it.

Start by putting it on a flat level surface with all the tyres inflated to the same pressure, say 20 pounds per square inch. Now lift the front and see if the front wheels can be rotated at the same time as they just clear the ground. You are roughly checking the front corner weights. Measure the distance from the top of the front kingpin (the bolt holding the stub axle to the chassis) to the middle of the rear axle, on each side. The distance should be within a millimetre or two. Try and measure diagonally from the front kingpin to the opposite rear bearing hanger. If any of these measurements are wildly different then the chassis is bent.

Spin the axle to make sure it is not bent. The chain tension should not vary much as you slowly turn the rear axle. Look carefully for cracks in the chassis, or evidence of cracks having been welded up. These often occur near the bearing hangers. Look underneath to see how much damage has been done riding the kerbs.

Check the brake. Is there plenty of pad material. Are they sticky or spongy. What about the seat? Remember you might have to buy a new seat to fit yourself anyway. But if it does fit, are there any cracks round the mounting holes.

Now for the engine. There should be invoices showing the recent rebuilds. It is quite usual to take the cylinder head and barrel off to inspect the insides. The bore should be clean with no score marks. The crank halves should not be damaged in any way. The piston rings should be free to move. As the engine wears, the cylinder is re-bored to take a larger size piston. Eventually the bore size becomes over the cubic capacity limit for the class, and an expensive new liner needs to be fitted. This is why you might see first bore as a selling point in the advert.

It is much more difficult to determine if the engine is legal for the class. In the economy classes the engines are not allowed much tuning. So the tuners try and work as close to the limit of the regulations as possible. Sometimes they go over and the engine is illegal, and virtually scrap. Unscrupulous people could try and off-load such engines on unsuspecting punters. Get a signed agreement stating that the engine is legal for the class, else you get your money back. It might be better than nothing.

If you are not familiar with karts, take someone with you who is. Even if you know what you are looking for, it is always better to have two pairs of eyes looking at a kart.

If you are there to buy your first kart, you are going to be led by your heart and be thinking, 'I've got to have it!' If you take someone with you who is slightly removed from that desire, they can prove to be a worthwhile calming influence.

Maybe your budget will run to a new kart. Then you will be visiting the dealers and manufacturers to view their latest creations. You have probably already short-listed a couple of makes. In some classes the maximum price for chassis and engine is fixed. Beware the special price for a factory engine. Sometimes this will have some basis in fact, especially in some gearbox classes, but more often not. Comer Cadet and TKM engines have to be blueprinted to bring them fully up to race specification. This is why a used engine with a good pedigree will command a higher price than a new one. Blueprinting need only cost a couple of hundred pounds maximum, and could be done at the first rebuild.

A good option in a class such as Formula TKM is to buy a second-hand chassis with a new engine. That way you know the history of the engine, and to begin with you will not notice the small difference blueprinting makes. If a driver is staying in the class he will want to keep his best engines anyway. If you need to buy new engines for a Prokart, then remember they have to be modified to remove the governors before racing. Doing this will, of course, completely negate the manufacturer's guarantee, but that's racing! In some classes, for instance Honda Cadet and Rotax, the engines are sealed and can only be serviced by approved dealers.

In some classes, notably Formula Junior TKM and Intermediate, there is a restrictor between the carburettor and the engine. This restricts the flow of petrol and air mix to the engine and limits the maximum power. In these classes the restrictor must be stamped with the manufacturers name.

In most classes there is a period, usually three years, with stability of engines or chassis or both. The equipment is either homologated or registered for the period, and during that period no new designs will be permitted. For international classes, the homologation is done by the CIK, and for national classes by the MSA. So find out when the homologation period expires, because it could lead to a sudden depreciation when the new kit comes in which could be quicker. On the other hand the last few months of a homologation period is a great time to pick up some good karts at a great price. The jump in performance is never as great as the drivers hope.

3.4 KART PREPARATION

The first aim of race kart preparation should always be to ensure conformity with the safety and technical regulations specified in the MSA Blue Book, the Gold Book or other class regulations. These documents will clearly state what can be done to the kart. If the regulations don't specifically say that something can be done, it probably can't! In all cases, follow these documents as your bible. Some of the following text may not be appropriate to all classes of racing - only a careful study of the technical regulations will identify just what is permitted.

PREPARATION

The most important aspect of kart preparation is to check, check and check again. There is simply no substitute for checking everything that can be checked as frequently as possible. The use of a printed check-list of items to be covered can be a good way of keeping on top of the situation, and ensuring that nothing vital is over-looked.

Go to a top championship meeting on a Saturday evening and under each awning the karts will be stripped right down, cleaned and rebuilt and then checked bolt by bolt ready for raceday. Occasionally drivers will take their engine to the scrutineer to have it's legality checked before racing commences.

A competition vehicle is, theoretically, driven on the limit all the time and so all of the components will have a much shorter life. It is very easy to under-estimate this so you need to be very aware of the stresses that are being put on components and cover all the basic things when looking at, and indeed preparing the kart.

Basic preparation will cover the essential safety items like wheel and axle bearings, brakes, steering and chain and sprocket covers. Brakes should be a number one priority when preparing the kart and make sure you

bleed the system properly. The brake pedal must not travel further than the top of the front bumper rail. Make sure the piston travel in the master cylinder is not excessive, if it is the pads need adjusting or renewing. On some calipers shims are inserted behind the pads as they wear, on others there are adjusting screws to take up the adjustment. Sometimes after adjustment the brake disc needs to be re-centred between the pads. Do not have too small a gap between the disc and the pads on the rear axle. Because the axle flexes going round corners the pads may bind and consume vital engine power if they are too close. Put a safety cable between the pedal and the master cylinder that will take effect if the brake rod snaps or a pin shears.

Look after your tyres. Take the wheels off the kart after the race, deflate the tyres, wash them clean and store them in a dark place with no extremes of temperature. When you mount new tyres be careful not to damage them. With a bit of practice you can demount a used tyre and mount a new tyre on a rim without use of tools. Some people advocate a tyre lubricant to make the tyre pop onto its seat easier. Others think this gives a greater chance of the tyre coming off the rim when racing.

In either case never over-inflate the tyre to get it to pop onto its seat. If possible, inflate the tyre within a correct size casing to keep the carcass from distension. Removing the tyre valve core when first inflating onto the rim will help. In long circuit racing and most International classes, it is mandatory to have pegs in the rims to keep the tyre seated. A tyre coming off the rim at 150mph is not a good thing. These are usually M5 or M6 cap screws inserted with plumbers tape for a seal. If you need to run low tyre pressures these pegs can be a useful aid in short circuit racing as well and are usually employed on the outer side of the rear wheels.

Depending on the class and the type of tyre, the slicks can be used for more than one meeting. At championship level almost everyone will have a new set of slicks for every meeting. In fact the regulations will only permit one set of slicks per meeting, plus one spare front and one spare rear if they have been damaged. Control tyres are often issued at championship meetings to ensure everyone gets the same compound and no cheating prevails. Doctoring the tyres is definitely not allowed, and the penalties are severe. But at club level the tyres may last several meetings. You may find a championship driver who is willing to sell you his once-used tyres at a large discount over the new price.

Wet weather tyres will quickly lose their edge on a drying track, and may overheat and go off. Because of this, some drivers will have an old set of wets mounted up on rims for just such an occasion, and keep their newest wets for really wet weather. Getting tyre pressures right on a drying track is critical. Looking after your wets may be even more important than your slicks, they may last you the whole season.

Front wheel and axle bearings need cleaning and lubricating if they are not the sealed kind. The rear axle should spin freely for a minute or more when the chain is removed and this will prove if the bearings are in alignment. Even with a chain and clutch connected the axle and drive system in a top driver's Cadet kart will spin freely, even for as long as five minutes.

To fit a new axle, or check the one already fitted, follow this procedure. Nip the bearing hanger bolts up so that the bearing can just be moved about. Check the measurement from the top of the front stub axle kingpin bolt to a point on the rear bearing and ensure it is the same plus or minus a millimetre or so on each side. Push the axle in from the engine side through any sprocket carriers, water pump pulleys (and belts) and the brake disc towards the opposite bearing. For the moment leave out any third bearing. Move the axle in the engine side bearing until it is central to the opposite side bearing and push it through. Continue pushing until it just comes out of the engine side bearing. Centralise the axle in the bearing if necessary and push it back into the engine side bearing.

Repeat the process until it is definitely central to each bearing from the opposite side. Tighten the bearing hanger bolts fully and re-check the axle rotates freely. Fit any third bearing and centralise it, then tighten its carrier bolts. Now insert the grub screws and pinch them up. Remove then one at a time, carefully centre punch the axle through the hole and drill a small way into the axle for at least one grub screw per bearing. Use a small amount of loctite and refit each grub screw. It is a good idea to wrap a little tape around each bearing over the grub screws, or use a tie-wrap, so that if the grub screws come loose they do not come out.

The chain needs to be cut to the correct length. To do this you need a chain-splitter tool to remove links until the chain is the correct length. Larger size chains often have a removable split link, but the links in smaller chains used in direct-drive need to be re-riveted. The chain tension should be set to give about 10mm of movement. Spray the chain with chain grease at regular intervals during a test or race day. The spray should be applied in advance of the race day to allow it to soak in. Clean the chain too after race days, especially wet ones.

When the engine is mounted on the chassis, temporarily tighten up the clamp bolts. Use a straight edge across the axle sprocket to the engine sprocket and adjust the axle sprocket carrier on the axle until the two sprockets are perfectly aligned. Then loosen the engine clamps and fit the chain, re-tensioning it to give free play of about 10mm.

Setting up the steering is important. Put the steering wheel in the straight ahead position and clamp it if possible. Set the rear wheels the same distance out from the rear bearing hangers and do likewise with the front wheels using the same amount of spacers each side. Using a long straight edge across the outer edge of each front wheel adjust the track rods so that the straight edge is crossing the rear tyre at the same point each side. Now check the toe-in or toe-out. A quick way to do this is to make a little cross on each tyre halfway across the tread surface. Put the crosses to the front three o'clock position and measure the distance between them. Then rotate the tyres so the crosses are at the rear nine o'clock position and measure again. The difference will be the toe. Experience and testing will give you the best position but it should be within a range of a couple of millimetres in or out.

See Chapter 5

Having earlier set the kart parallel, make any adjustments equally to each track rod. When you can afford to, buy a set of front set up plain discs which replace the front wheels for set up of toe and camber.

Are the chain and sprocket covers in place? The scrutineer will not pass the kart if your fingers can touch the engine sprocket. The chain guard is there to protect both you and a following driver should your kart throw its chain. Make sure the seat is fixed securely, and the exhaust system has no leaks.

You may have to add ballast to bring the combined weight of yourself and your kart up to the minimum weight for the class. Add lead ballast until the weight is one or two kilos over the limit with a nearly empty tank, and you should be okay. Later you can shave the weight nearer the limit. Each piece of ballast must be securely fixed with two bolts and no single piece can weigh more than 5kg.

Drain the fuel after each meeting, especially if your machine is a two-stroke. Petroil does not keep well unless stored in a sealed container so you should use a fresh mixture of racing two-stroke oil and super unleaded fuel for each meeting. Sixteen to one is the usual mixture (half a pint of oil to a gallon of fuel) but less oil may be optimum with some types of oil or engine. As super unleaded may become harder to source, special (but legal) fuel will be available from suppliers like ATOL. Some classes like TKM will run perfectly happily on normal premium unleaded.

If the engine is brand new it will need running in. It will also need running in if it has been fitted with a new piston, and to a lesser extent if other new parts have been fitted. To run in a two-stroke go out in ten minute sessions and only rev the engine to about two-thirds of normal peak revs. Take the engine up to that point, then choke the carburettor air intakes to richen the mixture, braking if necessary, then repeat the process. Gradually over a few sessions, increase the speed and decrease the frequency of choking to about three or four times a lap until anything from 15 to 30 minutes of running in has been achieved. Your engine supplier will advise how long.

Some modern pistons can stand less time, the important thing is to follow your engine builder's instructions. The engine builder may have undertaken some of the running-in on a dyno, leaving you the requirement to only have one slower running-in session. Each time you come in from a session, check the mixture. If it is not a sealed engine, before you finally go up to racing speed you might remove the barrel and check the piston has no remaining high spots, and the top edge of the piston is not showing any marks of touching the head, leaving the top ring free to move.

A critical factor in two-strokes is the squish clearance. This is the gap between the top of the piston at top dead centre and the cylinder head. It might be between 50 and 60 thousands of an inch for a less highly tuned engine, down to 30 thou for a highly tuned category. It is measured by squashing a length of solder inserted through the plug hole and turning the engine over top dead centre. Too small and the piston will be ruined. Another cause of piston damage is detonation, when the petrol/air mixture is not burning evenly. This can cause small chips or even holes in pistons. Incorrect ignition timing can cause detonation.

Once the engine is run-in and you are up to speed, keep checking the mixture. Look at the piston crown, either with a small torch through the plug hole, or by removing the cylinder head. A dry black/grey colour is correct. Light grey or white signifies too weak a mixture, and a danger of seizure. Wet, black and oily is too rich, will cause the plug to foul up and will prevent the engine from achieving full revs. It will tend to four-stroke at higher revs rather than run cleanly. Reading the plug will also indicate the mixture. So long as the correct plug type in the heat range is being used, then the ceramic under the spark gap should be a light tan colour, and the outer metal a dull black. Too cold a plug type will make starting difficult, and too hot or soft a plug may overheat in a long race. Sometimes a softer plug is used in wet weather conditions.

Some carburettors, typically fitted to 100cc engines, will have an adjustable low and high jet. Ask your dealer for the initial settings for these. Gearbox and four-stroke engines usually only have carburettors with interchangeable jets. Start with a conservative setting, on the rich side, then change to lean down until the mixture is correct. The engine will be quickest with the correct setting, not too rich, and will overheat and lose power if too lean even if it does not seize. In some classes, like Honda four-strokes, only certain jet sizes are permitted. Fixed jets will have a number stamped on them, a jet with a smaller number allows less fuel through, hence the expression jetting-down to weaken the mixture.

The simple carbs on Cadets and 100cc karts can be fitted with a carb kit, a set of gaskets and other parts to rejuvenate a tired carb. When stripping and rebuilding a carb, it must be carried out in conditions of spotless cleanliness. Parameters such as float chamber and delivery valve lever heights are critical. Routinely check that fuel filters are not clogged.

If you are unlucky enough to have a seize it may be anything from a slight nipping-up to a full blown catastrophic failure with the piston welded firmly to the liner. If it has just nipped up you may be able to free it off by polishing with a fine wet and dry or crocus paper to keep you going. Ensure the rings are free to move, otherwise you will need to clean up the seats as well. However the aluminium from the piston will also have transferred to the liner, so it will need to be honed or re-bored on a specialist machine and a new piston fitted at the earliest opportunity.

Engine life will depend on the class. A Formula TKM two-stroke or JICA engine should run for five or six hours between major rebuilds but a faster 100cc engine may only safely last two or three hours. At the other extreme, a Rotax Max maybe up to 50 hours if carefully maintained. Prokart engines need little attention except for regular oil changes and it may sometimes be more cost-effective to buy a new engine than have an extensive rebuild. To put this in perspective a typical race meeting will use 35 to 40 minutes of life. It is testing which gobbles up engine life, or Enduro racing.

Good kart preparation is all about attention to detail. You need to put the time and effort in and, if necessary, you may need to get some help in from other sources, especially for engine maintenance. Good preparation is not necessarily about spending money, either. Time is the critical factor.

If you have just bought your first kart, allow yourself plenty of time to prepare it. Do not be tempted into rushing into your first race because if you are not properly prepared, you may well end up wasting a lot of time and money.

3.5 TESTING

Before the first race, go out in a number of test sessions. That way, you can locate any potential faults on the kart at a time when you are not under pressure to complete a race. Inevitably, when you do start racing, you will want to at least finish the races and start getting signatures on your racing licence.

During a test session, you can go out and do a few laps and if you're not sure about something, you can come back into the pits and sort it out. Equally, as the driver, you can build yourself up gradually as you explore the kart's capabilities away from the pressure of a race meeting.

Just as you should give yourself plenty of time when looking around to buy a kart, do the same as you prepare towards your first race. Allow ample time to work through the kart before the first test and then allow more time to carry out some testing before you plan to race it for the first time. It may be worthwhile, even before you select the kart, to sit down and make a timetable to plan what you are going to do at what stage, especially as your local track may only have occasional test days. Your target will be your first race!

Just how long the various stages of preparation will take can vary enormously depending on the type of kart you plan to race, what knowledge you have and what resources are available to you. But the thing that drivers invariably find is that they run out of time as the first scheduled race draws near. Going into your first race ill-prepared will invariably lead to disappointment or, perhaps, much worse.

An old adage that holds good in this situation is that if you are failing to plan, you are planning to fail. Setting yourself sensible targets and then keeping to them will add professionalism to your racing and, ultimately help make it more enjoyable and, hopefully, more successful.

Before a test day, sit down and work out a plan for the entire day of what you are going to do and what you hope to achieve. During the day, you may have to revise the plan, but at least at the start of the day you know what you are trying to achieve. This should ensure that you are covering specific areas and are not just working on a hit and miss basis. Testing does not come cheaply and it is important to make the best use of valuable track time.

See Chapter 8.2

Once you have become familiar with the kart and feel you are getting near the pace, try and keep testing to short runs of perhaps six laps at a time. Then, come back to the pits and analyse what happened in those laps so that when you next go out, you have specific things that you are trying to achieve with your driving and set-up. You should try varying the adjustable parameters on the kart one at a time so you can feel the difference each makes.

However, in the early stages of your racing, you will be so busy with just driving the kart that you will probably not be aware of all the other things that are going on around you. For instance, simply by changing sprockets, you could find half a second per lap improvement immediately.

When you go testing, set yourself sensible targets. Ask the person you bought the kart from for the gearing and basic set up details. This will give you a base point to work from and could also save you pounding round and round, trying to figure out what to do and which gear to use. Don't try and go fast too soon, cold slick tyres do not provide much grip, but properly inflated hot slicks are very sticky. To begin with you are in a chicken and egg situation, you are not going fast enough to generate heat in the tyres, thus making you more likely to spin. Put a few extra pounds in the tyres to make them warm up more quickly.

Recently, a driver borrowed a more powerful kart from a team with a view to stepping up a class. He went out in the kart and tried much too hard too soon. On just his third lap of the test session, he made a mistake and crashed heavily, leaving the kart badly damaged.

The result: damage totalling many hundreds of pounds, a disillusioned team and a driver who may now drop out of the sport. It is not a unique story, but could easily have been avoided with a steady build up for kart and driver.

An added advantage of doing some testing before your first race is that you should have less of a culture shock when you then arrive for your first race. You must not just buy a kart and turn up for your first race.

It is not uncommon for a new driver to buy a kart and turn up for their first test session (hopefully not a race) with a mental picture of their own driving capabilities putting them somewhere in the middle of the field. However, they suddenly find that they are three seconds a lap slower than even the next slowest kart in the race. Then, they've got a much bigger mountain to climb than if they'd taken time to prepare themselves and built up to a sensible speed before entering their first race.

By learning some of the ropes before the first race, you have a better chance of finishing in the middle of the pack. At least then the leaders will be in sight! Of course, not everyone who goes racing does it purely to win. In any race, there can only be one winner from, perhaps 20 to 60 karts in the class. Other drivers race for the pleasure and excitement of doing it, and there is no disgrace in finishing further down the order. In every race, someone must finish last.

The target for your first race should, therefore, be to finish without being hopelessly out-classed by the rest of the field and not to do anything silly. Do not expect to win your first race. It may happen in your dreams, but is incredibly unlikely in reality.

If you draw a parallel with a sport like golf, you would not expect to buy a set of clubs, teach yourself how to use them, and then turn up at a competition and win, having never been round the course before. So why should anyone expect motor racing to be any different?

The problem with motor racing in this respect, is that most people can drive a road car before they start racing. But the two activities are so well removed from each other that many people cannot believe the difference once they start racing. People who think they drive fast on the road are in for a big shock if they think racing will simply be an extension of that. There is a lot to learn and you can't learn it all in your first test session.

3.6 MENTAL AND PHYSICAL PREPARATION FOR THE DRIVER

Proper mental and physical preparation for the driver is vital to the outcome of the race. It can be the difference between winning and losing, or having a good race or a bad race. First of all, you need to be reasonably fit, depending upon the type of kart you are planning to race. The medical examination before you gained your licence will have ensured a basic level of health, but what many drivers find tiring is the mental side of racing, the concentration that is needed.

PREPARING PHYSICALLY

When driving on a circuit, even after as little as half a dozen laps, you can feel very drained. Race driving demands a level of concentration that people are not used to. We all drive on the road in quite a relaxed fashion and seldom concentrate 100%. In a race kart, there is nothing but pure concentration. That is what tires a lot of people.

Above and beyond that, is the actual stress of driving a racing kart on a circuit and the pressure you put on yourself. The adrenalin is pumping and everyone finds it very tiring, especially in the early days of a racing career. You need to be able to build yourself up to that very gradually by doing some form of mental exercise to improve your levels of concentration.

Ultimately, you should be trying to develop the ability to overcome the emotion and stress of a racing situation and take a more clinical approach. This will help you perform to the best of your ability but is not a skill that is easily mastered. Many drivers suffer from inconsistent performances, one race battling for the lead and the next struggling in the midfield. Invariably, this is down to mental condition and concentration, rather than variations in kart performance.

When you are driving quickly, it is important to be able to understand why that is the case and, conversely, when you are not going so well, be able to pinpoint what changes you need to make. In terms of physical preparation, it is strongly advisable not to drink alcohol at all in the lead up to a race. Ideally, allow plenty of time for any alcohol to completely clear out of your system. It is worth noting that the race officials are able to carry out random tests on the morning of a race meeting to check for any driver under the influence of alcohol or drugs.

Recently, a driver attended a barbecue on the Saturday evening before a race meeting and drank several pints of beer. The following morning he was selected for a random blood test and proved to still be over the specified limit. Not only was he excluded from the race meeting, but was fined and had his racing licence endorsed.

It is, of course, utter folly to attempt to race when under the influence of alcohol or drugs. You risk not only your own life, but those of your fellow competitors and race organisers will quite correctly come down very heavily on anyone transgressing. Equally, if you have invested time and effort in your kart, you would not deliberately do something to hinder its performance. So, why do the same thing to the driver?

Take time to create the right driving position, for this is the office environment when you are racing. If you are not comfortable and in the correct position, your performance will suffer. The ideal driving position is to have the knees bent a little, and be able to depress the pedals to the limit without stretching. The seat should be a tight fit and you should be able to move the steering wheel without your elbows banging into parts of the kart or engine. Your hands should be on the steering wheel at the classic ten to two or quarter to three position with the arms bent.

Practice reaching for any adjustments such as the choke control, if any, or the carburettor jet adjustments. If you are driving a kart with a clutch, make sure the engine kill switch is comfortably to hand and works. It must be marked with its OFF position. If racing a gearbox kart, is the gearlever a comfortable reach and movement?

Practice starts, but only in a safe place. Also practice restarting the kart on your own if it should spin and stall the engine. One or two classes have electric starters but this is rare. Normally you need to be pushing the kart, and jump in to catch the engine firing before the speed drops away. Quite an art, but practice will make the difference between a finish and non-finish.

In the lead up to a race, you should try and spend some time focusing on what you will be doing on the day of the race. Part of that preparation should be to ensure that your body is in the best condition possible for the rigours of racing. During the race, particularly in warmer weather, you will lose body fluids and so you should stock up on suitable fluids accordingly. Kart racing on a hot day can be a sweaty business.

The exact quantity to drink is very much down to the individual and you most certainly do not want to finish the race with your legs crossed having drunk too much liquid before the race! Trial and error is the best way, but you will find many drivers drinking copious amounts of mineral water or sports drinks immediately after the race.

Just as drinking alcohol can slow your reactions, so can excessive food. A sensible approach is to limit breakfast to cereals and toast. If you do have some lunch in the course of the day, try and eat in plenty of time before your next race so that your body has time to digest the food. The key is plan the day and meals accordingly. If you are having particular problems, or want to take the matter further, it is best to seek professional advice.

The other thing that racing drivers should avoid the night before a race is sex! This will be more of a problem to some drivers than others and is best left to personal decision.....

The level of personal fitness required to race successfully will vary from class to class and in the entry-level classes, you need not be superfit to race successfully. However, regular exercise is beneficial to every day life as well as racing. Cardio-vascular exercise is always useful, as is any activity that helps increase your stamina. If you progress higher up the racing ladder, you will almost certainly need to work on fitness as upperbody and neck muscles will come under increasing strain as cornering speeds increase.

Top level drivers are among the fittest of all sportsmen. If you feel this is an area you could improve, you should consider working with a fitness trainer who is qualified to show you exercises that will suit your particular situation. Any local gym should be able to provide you the name of a professional trainer.

3.7 DRIVER COACHING

The hardest thing for many drivers to admit is that a lack of front-running speed may be down to the driver and not the kart. The Racing Drivers Book of Excuses is an oft-quoted mythical publication that, if ever written, would run to many hundreds of pages!

There are many ways of approaching your first race. A route chosen by some aspiring racers is to spend lots of time testing, preferably with a team or ARKS School Instructor building up their confidence and speed with tuition and one to one driver coaching. Then, when they arrive at their first race, they are on the pace straightaway and comfortable with their new surroundings.

This does not have to be the case, however, and there are a lucky few who have sufficient natural ability to be able to jump straight into a kart and run competitively with little or no coaching. But, let's face it, they are the exception and not every driver is going to be the next Michael Schumacher. Indeed, many of them have no particular wish to be a Grand Prix star.

Others turn up for their first meeting without much of a clue about what they are doing and find that they are completely lost. They don't know their way around the track, don't know the lines to use and are a danger to themselves as well as the rest of the competitors. This is when personal frustration can set in. Equally, they can then waste a lot of money thinking that the scope for improvement must be in the chassis or the engine.

However, they should really be looking inside the seat for the source of the problem. Does the driver know what he is doing? If you are three seconds a lap off the pace at your first meeting, the chances are that those three seconds are in the driver and not the equipment.

It might even be possible to have your coach or instructor drive your kart and set it up for you. The instructor will set a target time to show you the kart's capability on the track. Although there is inevitably a cost involved in enlisting the support of a driver coach, it could prove to be very cost-effective. Consider the alternatives. First, you invest more money in the equipment, perhaps an engine rebuild or some development work which may prove to be largely worthless. Second, in frustration at your relative lack of speed, you start trying too hard and run the risk of having an accident as you try and find the time you are losing.

Not everyone will use a coach, and we don't suggest that it is an essential step in the learning process. But, if you are struggling to match the pace of your rivals, time spent with a coach - who will probably charge about £150 per day - may just be the most cost-effective way of getting to the root of your problems. If you talk to any driver who has had proper professional coaching, they will rate the benefits very highly. One day with a good coach could teach you more than two seasons of racing.

Another time to consider coaching is when you feel you have reached a plateau in your own performance, and are not making any real forward progress. Of course, if you are now winning races by a lap, it could be that there is no further room for improvement, but this is seldom the case!

DRIVER COACHING

A good coach should, in most cases, be able to help you move forward from that plateau to the next level of performance. It is fair to say that some very experienced drivers have faults to which they are oblivious. A number of Grand Prix drivers work with coaches and, if you consider a sport like tennis or golf, even the very best players in the world have coaches.

Taking this a stage further, nowadays many karts are fitted with some form of data-logging system which records what is happening to the kart on each lap in considerable detail. The analysis of this data has become a major part of the work of professional and semi-professional teams and drivers.

However, you need to be able to interpret the data you are gathering. It is now fashionable to have this equipment in karts but before you invest in the kit, make sure you have a way of understanding the data you are collecting. If you are inexperienced, you could end up confusing yourself.

 *See Chapter 5.8*

If working with a driver coach who is also driving your kart, you will then be able to overlay data and draw very specific conclusions about where and why you are losing time on the circuit.

CHAPTER 4
THE FIRST RACE MEETING

IN THIS CHAPTER

4.1 ENTERING YOUR FIRST RACE
- ➤ Club memberships
- ➤ Championships
- ➤ Entry forms

4.2 TESTING: WHEN WHERE AND HOW MUCH?
- ➤ How often to test
- ➤ Where to go testing
- ➤ Be prepared to travel
- ➤ Making the most of track time

4.3 THE FIRST RACE DAY
- ➤ Entry confirmation
- ➤ Planning the day
- ➤ The paperwork
- ➤ Signing-on
- ➤ Scrutineering
- ➤ Drivers briefing

4.4 PRACTICE
- ➤ Official practice
- ➤ Starting your kart
- ➤ Timed qualifying
- ➤ Heats and finals

4.5   TEAM HELP

> ➤ Pushers
>
> ➤ Timing
>
> ➤ Noise checks

4.6   THE RACE BUILD-UP

> ➤ Dummy grid
>
> ➤ Race starts
>
> ➤ False starts

4.7   RACE DRIVING

> ➤ Smoothness is the key
>
> ➤ The first corner
>
> ➤ Being lapped
>
> ➤ Choking the carb

4.8   WET WEATHER RACING

> ➤ Driving in the rain
>
> ➤ Aquaplaning
>
> ➤ Changing conditions
>
> ➤ Visibility - or lack of it
>
> ➤ Wet weather attire
>
> ➤ Tyre choice

4.9   PARADE CARS, PACE CARS, SAFETY CARS AND SAFETY PERIODS

> ➤ Use of parade cars and pace cars
>
> ➤ Use of safety cars and karts
>
> ➤ The black and yellow flag
>
> ➤ The red flag and restarts

4.10 OVERTAKING AND DEFENDING

➤ Types of passing move

➤ The planned move

➤ The opportunist move

➤ Defending fairly

➤ Slipstreaming

4.11 LOSING CONTROL

➤ Building up to your limit

➤ The first spin

➤ Safe re-starting

➤ Avoiding spinning karts

➤ Getting onto the grass

➤ If you have a shunt

➤ The role of the marshals

4.12 AFTER THE CHEQUERED FLAG

➤ The slowing-down lap

➤ Getting back into the paddock

➤ Plug-chops and checking the temperature

➤ Parc ferme and weighing

➤ Raised tempers

➤ De-briefing

➤ Check the results

➤ Packing up and prize-giving

➤ Enjoyment

4.1 ENTERING YOUR FIRST RACE

By now you will have chosen a class and joined a club that regularly races that class at their meetings.

See Chapter 7

Typically, racing membership of a kart club will cost between £20 and £50 for the year. After mid-season there may be a discount through to the end of the year. Later, when you progress to entering a championship, you may need to register or even pre-qualify. There will be additional fees for these. Every championship is required to have a co-ordinator and for some of the higher-profile championships, this is almost a full time occupation but still likely to be a volunteer doing the job in their spare time. With club championships you are automatically entered when you join the club. Usually there will need to be a minimum number regularly racing in a class before a club championship will be set up.

Each club will publish its SRs, Supplementary Regulations, and its Championship Regulations even just for the club championship. Get hold of these and study them carefully. The SRs will cover any special rules the club employs, perhaps additional silencing regulations. The championship regulations will show how points are scored. Maybe only those finishing in the A Final will score points, or it might go down to the last finisher.

Next you need to get hold of an entry form for your first race. The club you joined may well have sent you some along with your membership card. Some clubs are very fussy and insist you use their own race entry forms, whereas others might accept another club's form. So it is always best to plan ahead by sending a stamped addressed envelope to the secretary or competition secretary of the club for an entry form well before the meeting.

Usually, entries for a particular meeting open well in advance of the meeting and close approximately one week before the date of the meeting or two weeks for a major championship race. You must send a stamped self-addressed envelope with your entry form and cheque so that the competition secretary can reply with your entry and race number confirmation. Most kart meetings do not need entry tickets, they assume anyone coming before 9am is driving or helping. After that time they will start charging for spectators.

Put your entry form in early, at least a week before the closing date. Popular classes fill up quickly and you might find your entry refused, or be put on a reserve list. Many clubs offer a system of leaving your entry for the following month's race at the previous meeting.

The entry forms are straightforward and cover the basic information that the organisers need.

Typically this will include:

- Your name, as you want to see it in the programme.
- Your address, with the town name you want to see in the programme.
- Your telephone number, in case they need to contact you at a late stage.
- Your racing class, and your preferred competition number.
- Your next of kin details.

When you join a club at the beginning of the season they may put your preferred number into a database so that you can keep that number all year. But if you go to another club, that number may already be in use, so the club will offer you an alternative. Be prepared to buy numbers on the day in that case. You must not choose numbers 0, or 1 through 15 in Class 1, or 1 through 9 in Class 4 as these are reserved for those who finish in that place in the previous year's national championships. Clubs generally do not allocate numbers over 99. Get a recent programme and look for an unused number in your class.

Next you need to put down your chassis make, and engine make, again this will be shown in the programme. Technically if you change your chassis or engine make before the race you must inform the Competition

Secretary in writing. Your competition licence number will be required, and the grade. When you are a novice you must show that on the form, because it affects where you are put in the grids for the heats. Next you put down which club you belong to and then sign and date the indemnity. If you are under 18, then your parent or guardian must sign also, and if they are not to be present on raceday then they need to issue a signed letter of authorisation to be carried by whoever is looking after you on the raceday. That person will act as your entrant.

One more part of the form is still to be completed. Your next of kin contact details are important in the unlikely event you are taken to hospital.

Kart clubs prefer cheques, with your competition number and address on the back. If your cheque bounces you run the risk of having your competition licence withdrawn. The MSA takes these matters very seriously. Some clubs will cash the cheques as they come in, others will wait until just after the meeting.

If, for some reason, you miss the closing date, you may still be able to arrange a late entry. But this will be at the discretion of the organisers and may be subject to a late entry surcharge. Some clubs have a policy of never accepting late entries as they will have printed the programme and worked out the grids for the heats.

Each circuit is licensed for a maximum number of starters by the MSA. This may vary depending on the class as the more powerful gearbox karts may not be permitted so many starters. Competition secretaries will juggle with the entries to fill each class grid as much as possible. They may amalgamate classes, or split off sub-classes or even have separate races for novices. When the grid is full, they will not be keen on having one or two extra entries, except as reserves. But if they get a whole lot more entries in a class they may be able to run extra heats and have a B Final. This is a last chance race for those that have not done so well in their heats, sometimes called a repechage, where the first four finishers go onto the last four places on the A Final grid. Often clubs allocate places on the first heat in the order that entries are received.

4.2 TESTING: WHEN, WHERE AND HOW MUCH?

The level of resource, both time and money, that you have will dictate the amount of testing you do. Some would say that if you can afford to test, do it; if you can't afford to test, then don't. Generally, the amount of testing that goes on increases as you move up the racing ladder. In Super One, dedicated test days are arranged at each circuit before the meeting and if you miss the test, you will struggle to be competitive at the race meeting. Teams sometimes arrive on the Thursday and test all the way through to raceday. Some of this time may be used to run-in the race engines. On the other hand some championships, especially those catering for juniors, might have testing restrictions and only allow testing the day before the meeting.

See Chapter 8.2

Basically, if you are learning about race driving, testing is essential to get you used to handling the kart at speed before being thrown into a competitive environment. There is no substitute to time in the kart and if you were, for instance, a tennis player, you would expect to train several times a week. At least!

But testing is also a way of spending considerable sums of money and so it should be balanced against available resources. Testing uses up far more engine life than racing. Although when you first start, it won't matter too much if your tyres are past their best. But when you are seriously setting up your kart for a race, you will need reasonably good tyres or the data you acquire will be pretty useless. This is one reason why Formula A is so expensive - you need to test on new tyres. Some circuits offer week day testing and if you have a proper job - and without one, you are going to struggle to go racing - getting time off on a regular basis is not going to be easy. Then, of course, you may have to explain to the wife why the family holiday to Spain is off this year because you have used up all your annual holiday going testing! But if Dad or Mum is paying then you will still need time off school, unless it is during the holidays. Top juniors often have private tutors so that they can test regularly!

The choice of where to test is influenced by several factors. Firstly, you will probably want to test at the circuit where you are going to be racing, particularly if you plan to test regularly through the season. Secondly, geographics will most certainly influence where you go. Most people will use their local track for testing whenever possible.

However, when selecting a venue for testing, try and look at the value for money you get. Testing is all about getting the maximum of undisturbed track time during the day. Some circuits in the middle of the country will be popular choices, but if there are so many karts attending, the number of sessions for each driver may be limited.

In actual fact there are so few tracks offering unlimited testing, your choice will be dictated by the track's test schedule. The new PF International track between Newark and Grantham is one which offers regular testing, but you must belong to Trent Valley Kart Club to take advantage. Gearbox karts are not permitted though. Others offering regular testing are Rye House in Hoddesdon, Whilton Mill near Daventry and Clay Pigeon near Yeovil.

Serious testing means noting down all the parameters each time you go out, even to the extent of ambient temperature, humidity, wind speed and direction. Track conditions will change as the day progresses and rubber is laid down, and you will need to keep your kart attuned to these changing conditions. There will never be as much rubber down on a test day as on a championship raceday, especially if there are classes using the stickiest rubber. But the trend of how you are having to change the kart should be apparent. Of course you may test all day on a dry track then raceday dawns wet and windy, or vice-versa.

What if you spin? Some classes of kart have clutches, so if the engine is still running, check the track for oncoming traffic and rejoin in a safe manner. If in a gearbox class kart, swiftly dipping the clutch will be essential to keep the engine running. However if you are in a direct drive kart without a clutch the engine will almost certainly stall. To rejoin means push-starting the kart once more.

Go to a safe place, certainly not on the race-circuit, warm the engine up, then try starting the kart yourself. It's not easy, but you do not want to be trying this for the first time during your first race. Make sure your slow running adjustment does not allow the engine to run without your foot on the throttle, runaway karts are not fun for other drivers or marshals. Pick up the rear of the kart with one hand on the back bumper and the other on the back of the seat. Run along with it, then simultaneously drop it to the ground and jump in, getting your foot on the throttle to make it start.

There are products called Easistart and Quickstart wheels which are fixed to the chassis member behind the seat, and drop down to raise the rear wheels above the ground. This makes it easier to push start the kart without the effort of lifting the rear wheels. Then a trigger is applied as you jump in, to drop the wheel and the kart to the ground. A throttle arrangement is incorporated.

4.3 THE FIRST RACE DAY

The entry confirmation and final instructions will normally arrive in the post mid-week preceding the race meeting. This is likely to be no more than a card confirming your competition number.

Typically you need to arrive and set up before 8am. At that time the signing-on will open so be early in the queue, then you can scrutineer early and sort out any last minute dramas. Use any spare time to walk round the circuit, noting entry and exit points, the grid positions and start line, and the position of marshals' posts. If you are new to the circuit, look for the tyre marks on the tarmac to help define the racing line into the corners but ignore the skid marks heading off the track.

At signing-on you will need to produce all your documents, including your racing licence and club membership cards. All of these items are essential but you still hear stories of drivers making frantic dashes back home to collect something that is missing. If you live some way from the circuit, you run the risk of not competing if you do not have all of the relevant paperwork with you. If your kart or engine has a logbook to comply with its class regulations then make sure you bring it along.

THE RACE MEETING

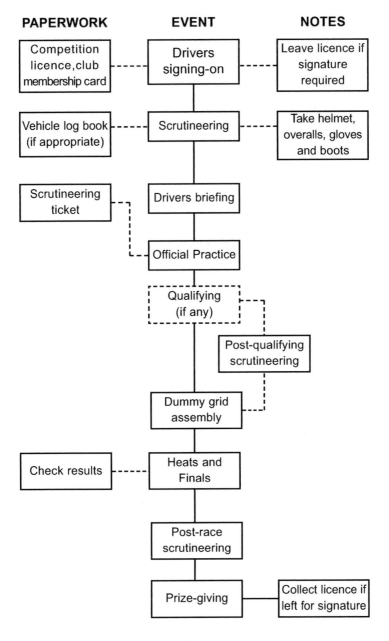

PAPERWORK	EVENT	NOTES
Competition licence, club membership card	Drivers signing-on	Leave licence if signature required
Vehicle log book (if appropriate)	Scrutineering	Take helmet, overalls, gloves and boots
Scrutineering ticket	Drivers briefing	
	Official Practice	
	Qualifying (if any)	
	Post-qualifying scrutineering	
	Dummy grid assembly	
Check results	Heats and Finals	
	Post-race scrutineering	
	Prize-giving	Collect licence if left for signature

Typically, there will be a queue at competitors' signing-on so allow some time in your schedule for this. If you are seeking novice or up-grading signatures on your racing licence, remember to leave the licence with the officials at this stage. The officials will give you a programme and a scrutineering card. Complete this with your chassis and engine serial numbers, and do not forget to put your name, class and competition number down also. Generally you are only allowed one chassis and two engines, but this will vary with different classes. Make sure you (and your guardian if you are under 18) sign the scrutineering card.

Next, you need to get your kart to the scrutineering bay so that the official scrutineers can make their safety inspections. The typical things that the scrutineers will be looking at closely include:

- Wheels, wheelnuts and tyres - are there any obvious defects, do they meet the regulations?

- Steering - is there any play, are the track rods free to move at all positions of lock?

- Drivers seat - is it safe and securely anchored?

- Engine cut-out switches for clutched engines - do they work as intended?

- Fuel tank - is it secure?

- Brakes, do they work properly - are there any obvious signs of leaking fluid or damaged lines?

- Helmet, racesuit, gloves and boots - do they meet current regulations?

- Exhaust and silencing system - is it secure and all joints tight?

- Chain and sprocket guard

- Ballast - is it secure and each piece fixed with two bolts?

They will check the kart against the basic kart technical regulations such as the bumper regulations and even those specifically for your class. But it is your responsibility to ensure your kart and engine is legal at all times. Ignorance of the regulations is no defence. Your kart will be more thoroughly checked for eligibility after the race if you finish high enough, or often just on a random basis.

The scrutineers will also check that critical items have lock nuts, and that a thread or two is showing through the lock nut. At big championship meetings your tyres may be marked, so that you can only use the one set, or a separate chassis seal may be fitted to positively identify your chassis. It is not unknown for certain teams to have different chassis for different conditions, but bearing the same serial number.

The official may keep your scrutineering card, marking you off on his list, or he may sign the card so that you can hand it in when you go for official practice.

Signing-on and scrutineering can take some time and there is a danger that you will find yourself running out of time before the start of the practice. Best advice is to allow even more time than you think is necessary and get to the circuit in good time.

Many teams prefer to arrive at the circuit the night before a race so that possible delays on the journey are eliminated. Clubs will usually have a place for tents, caravans or motorhomes. Many clubs reserve paddock spaces for their club members who pay extra for the privilege. These places will be marked out and numbered so do not park in them unless you want to uproot just before going out to practice.

If you can, when you are doing your research at race meetings about which class to contest, try and familiarise yourself with the paddock layout and the position of things like the signing-on office and scrutineering bay. This will all save valuable time on race day. If in any doubt, ask. Your fellow racers will usually be happy to point you in the right direction.

You will probably find the time between scrutineering (for which there will usually be a queue) and practice tending to evaporate. Therefore, it is sensible to have the kart ready for practice before going to scrutineering.

Things like changing tyres, fuelling up and so on are best done before scrutineering. Then, should you hit a snag at scrutineering and have to fix a last minute problem, you don't have to worry about the routine items.

After scrutineering go and weigh yourself plus the kart to ensure the scales of the day match your guess at the right amount of ballast. Some drivers weigh as they come in from practice but this often leads to yet another queue.

If you do have problems at scrutineering, do not lose your temper with the officials. They are, in some ways, there to protect racing drivers from themselves. If they pick you up on a particular point, it is for your own safety, either physically or to protect your licence should your kart fail eligibility. There is little point trying to dispute their verdicts on safety matters, it is up to you to be prepared and get the problem fixed to their satisfaction.

You are always looking to buy yourself as much time as possible so that when you are called up for practice, you have plenty of time in hand and you are well prepared. It is very easy to run out of time to do all the things that need to be done before you and the kart are ready to take to the track.

It is useful to display the meeting timetable somewhere prominently around your team (on the side of the tow van, for instance), so that everyone can check at a glance how much time you have and when your practice, heats and final are due. The really professional teams mount a dry-wipe board inside the transporter or awning with all relevant times noted and often have a large clock attached for good measure!

Finally, in the rush and excitement to get the kart ready to go onto the track, you must never forget about the safety of anyone working on it. Fuel is flammable and mixing it with oil is a hazardous occupation. Recently someone burnt down their awning and the nearby circuit perimeter fence by mixing their fuel in the awning which was being heated by a parafin heater. You must carry a suitable fire extinguisher in accordance with the 'Gold Book' regulations.

Remember that programme you were given when signing-on? It will have the time of the drivers' briefing, and the order of practice. Get to drivers' briefing in plenty time, there are hefty fines for anyone late or missing it. The Clerk of the Course will introduce himself or herself and their fellow senior officials. The Clerk will cover any particular points about the days racing and the track situation. They will emphasise the need to obey flag signals. Novice drivers will often be asked to remain after the general briefing, so that they can be more specifically briefed on the circuit and start procedure. Junior drivers and their helpers or pushers may also be asked to remain behind so that the pushers can be briefed where to stand on the track, if indeed this is permitted. Such pushers will have to sign on and be issued with a tabard for identification. They may need to pay a small deposit for the tabard.

4.4 PRACTICE

Official practice is your last chance to make sure all systems are working before your first race. Maybe you need to scrub in your new slicks. Hopefully you will not be attempting to finish running in the motor after a hasty overnight rebuild. In any case do not attempt to start your engine in the pits before practice, most clubs have strict rules about running engines in the pits.

When the engine is cold, it will need choking to start it up. With a two-stroke, before you leave your pits bring the petrol through to the carb by rocking the engine to pulse the pump. If you temporarily take off the air-filter you can hold your hand across the carburettor bell mouth until a small amount of petrol appears whilst rocking the engine. This will help to start a cold engine. If the carb has a choke, remember to apply it before attempting to start. If there is no choke then you need to hold your gloved hand across the air intake to artificially choke the engine whilst being push-started. As soon as it fires, take your hand off a little, and dab it back if the engine seems like it needs more choke. But be careful not to over-choke the kart, because you will quickly oil up the spark plug. Once the engine is firing take your hand off the intake, or switch off the choke after half a lap, and apply throttle to clear the engine.

The most critical requirement is to safely complete three laps, as this is the mandatory minimum to qualify you to race. If you fail to do three laps, you are at the mercy of the Clerk of the Course. Depending upon the timetable for the meeting, he may allow you to do three laps in a later practice session but ask permission straight away.

This short practice session is for you to check all the systems on the kart and see if your set-up is working. Since this is still early in the day track conditions will change but your team will want to hear your impressions of the handling. If you have not raced or practised at the circuit before, on the first lap out of the pits take a good look at the circuit conditions, and pay particular attention to the marshals' posts and the starting grid position. All of them will be displaying a green flag for the opening lap of the session to remind you of their position. However, even more important to check is whether any of them are displaying any other information, such as an oil flag. Be very cautious if the track still has damp patches, it is very easy to spin on cold wet tyres.

Generally, your first flying lap is not the most important one of the session and by taking the first couple of laps fairly steadily you will be able to bring kart, driver, tyres and brakes up to working temperature! You may also be scrubbing in brand new slicks, ready for racing later.

Some tracks have a different route used for the rolling laps or even the first racing lap, for instance missing out a chicane, so find out if this is so and look for that route whilst out in practice.

At certain meetings you might have timed qualifying to determine your grid position. For novices this means they do not necessarily have to start at the back of the grids in the heats, the grid place for everyone is determined by their best qualifying lap time. If transponders are used, as increasingly they will be, then there could be a large number of karts on the track together. Alternatively perhaps three or four karts will be sent out with gaps between for manual or beam timing.

If the former, try and find some clear track during qualifying. Frequently, you will hear drivers complain of traffic during qualifying. The number of karts on the track meant that they had been unable to get a clear lap in which to really push for a time. Racing around in a group during qualifying may be great fun, but it will seldom produce a good lap time.

Frequently, you will see experienced drivers coasting around during a session, looking for a gap in the traffic. If you chose to do this, be very aware of karts coming up behind you quickly and stay well off the racing line. Ruining someone else's hot lap while trying to find space for your own will probably earn you some harsh words in the paddock.

If you are with a small group you may get one warm up lap and only two timed laps. You need to be quick in both, but the first must be driven slightly more conservatively just in case you come off and get no time at all. Racing at the highest level, some British championship classes employ timed practice because it is good experience if you progress to European championship level. At club level there simply isn't the time for all to have timed qualifying, and anyway karting is all about overtaking and gaining grid position through the heats.

If not before, when you come in, look for your grid positions in the heats. Sometimes this will already be published in your programme, but it may be posted on the noticeboard. Even if it is in the programme amendments may be posted because of no-shows or late arrivals. Mark your position and your races and get to the grid in plenty of time.

You will likely have two or three heats. As a novice you will start from the back with the other novices in all the heats. The others will have a combination of a front, middle and back position or some other positions that add up to the same thing. To check this out, take the competition number of the polesitter in the first heat. Count that as a one. Then look for that same number in the other heats and add up all that kart's grid positions. Look at any other kart in the same race and their total grid positions should add up to the same number, plus or minus one. This is how you check if your grid positions are fair.

The key to successful qualification through the heats to the final is passing and gaining position on the others. Note that if you are on pole, you cannot gain position, only lose places. A pole will be counted as a zero points score, second as two points and so on with non-finishers getting the total grid plus one. It may seem obvious but non-finishing will not aid your progress up the grid.

4.5 TEAM HELP

Hopefully, you will have encouraged some friends or family to come along to the meeting and help out. There are many useful jobs they can do, especially helping to take your kart up and down to the grid and timing you on the race-track. If your kart is fixed drive without a clutch it will need to be push-started and you will need help.

You must be sitting in the kart with your foot on the brake before attempting to start a clutched engine. Either it will have a pull-start, a built-in electric start, or need a portable electric starter that engages the crankshaft. If the kart needs push-starting, ask two of your friends to push you off. If it is a gearbox class kart, dip the clutch and engage second or third gear, then let out the clutch to spin the engine. You will learn to jump down in the seat at the moment of disengaging the clutch to stop the rear wheels locking up as the engine hits compression. On a gearbox kart, only apply a small amount of throttle to avoid over-gassing the engine.

Other types of kart are equipped with carburettors less sensitive to the throttle opening. If it is a two-stroke direct drive kart your friends should pick up the rear of the kart by lifting the rear bumper, run along with it to gain speed then drop it whilst still pushing until the engine fires. You need to remember to dab the air intake or apply the choke. Your pushers must run off diagonally to the side of the track to avoid being run over by following traffic.

If the driver is a junior then some tracks will allow junior pushers on the track during testing and racing as a safety aid. The job of the junior pusher is to help the young driver get his or her kart quickly to a safe place following a spin, then re-starting the kart. During a race the pusher must help any driver, not just their own son or daughter. Before venturing onto the track, they must sign on and be equipped with a tabard to show their status. They may have to stand in a designated area.

Once equipped with a couple of stop-watches, your pit crew can gather valuable information. Pit boards are seldom used except in long circuit karting. During testing it is useful to agree a few hand signals, especially one to signal you in. Your helper or mechanic will time you and probably the fastest kart in your class, or maybe your main rival. Most watches come with memories these days so the times can be recalled later. Your mechanic will also be observing the handling of the kart, to compare this with your own impressions. This is where an experienced mechanic or instructor can really make the difference in setting your kart up to suit the conditions.

If you have been to the track before, perhaps for testing, and are now suddenly a second a lap slower, seeing the best times from other drivers will help you assess whether the track is slower for everyone or if you are losing time. Many circuits will vary from day to day in the lap times that are possible and you will hear talk of fast and slow days. Many factors can have an impact on this.

Ambient temperatures, the amount of rubber and oil on the track and weather conditions can affect the circuit. Of course, if you are going slower but no-one else is, you have a problem either with the kart or the driver which you need to address before the next race.

More and more tracks will be investing in transponder timing. By 2001 it will be expected that every driver will own a transponder with a unique number. At such tracks there may be a TV display of the lap times and race positions, or the times may be published afterwards. If you have invested in a data logging or hot-lap system of some sort, you will have your lap times displayed in front of you. You may also be able to purchase a display to sit on your steering wheel which shows and stores the lap times. In some classes these are not permitted for racing, only unofficial practice.

See Chapter 5.8

While the pit crew may be able to give you some information, you are largely on your own in a kart race and must be able to work out much of what is going on for yourself. Knowing your rivals and their numbers can help and, particularly in shorter races, just having a good look around you will tell you much of what you need to know. Some circuits lend themselves to looking across a corner to see who is where, but be careful not to miss your braking point while watching the leaders having a great battle! On the whole, it is best not to look back, ever. Concentrate on racing and the line ahead.

If you are likely to be lapped during a race, it is also worth taking a close look at the karts towards the front of the grid. Then, when they come up behind, you will be ready to keep out of their way when you see the blue flag.

In karting, outside assistance is not allowed for seniors once you are past the safety line, a white line painted across the track soon after the grid exit. If your kart breaks down after this point you have to use your own resources to get going again. The engine may fire for a short while then stop because of an oiled up spark plug. Some drivers carry a spare plug and plug spanner, but these must be securely fastened to the kart, or be in a bag securely fastened to the kart in at least two places. Carrying tools on your body is strictly forbidden. Junior pushers will usually take a plug and plug spanner out with them to aid any stranded youngsters.

Finally, clearly signal your intention to go into the pits by putting your hand up clearly and slow down. At the end of the practice session, if you have not already checked, go and weigh yourself and your kart to ensure you are over the class minimum. If you make any major changes to the kart during the day, such as a change from wets to slicks or an engine change, check the weight again. There is nothing so embarrassing as to fail the weight check, especially if you have finished well. Additionally you may earn an unwanted licence endorsement.

Quite possibly the environmental scrutineers will have been checking the noise from each kart during practice. Should you be unlucky enough to be called up, or worse still black-flagged, then you need to do something to quieten the kart before going out again. Remember if you are given the black flag you must see the Clerk of the Course.

The noise from the karts is measured with an overhead microphone suspended above the track where karts are producing maximum power (not necessarily maximum revs.). The maximum limit is 105dBA with the microphone at 3.6m high, or scaled measurements for alternative heights. Some clubs may set more stringent levels. The faster air-cooled 100cc classes may need an acoustic cover over the engine in order to pass the test, as well as rubber inserts between the fins or a couple of broad strips of silicon. It is quite difficult to quieten an air-cooled engine, as so much of the noise escapes directly out of the cylinder barrel and crankcase. A water-cooled engine is much easier to make quiet, by the use of efficient mufflers and air intake boxes. Water-cooled engines are freely available for Formula 100 National, ICA and Formula A, and will increasingly become the norm in all 100cc classes. Nearly all gearbox class engines are water-cooled.

4.6 THE RACE BUILD-UP

After practice you may not have very long before your first heat is called to the grid. If you have had timed qualifying, you will need to keep an eye out for the publication of the grid sheets. Make time for any changes to the kart settings, remembering to note down any setting changes you make for future reference.

As a matter of routine, you should have checked that there is enough fuel in the kart, that tyre pressures are correct and that the wheel nuts are properly torqued up. You should also check the mixture by looking at the spark plug or top of the piston. If it is too dry (pale whitish colour) you risk running too lean and seizing the engine. You will, of course, have found out how many laps are in the race, so as to estimate the amount of fuel required. If you don't take the kart to the grid yourself, it is worth making sure that your helmet, gloves and balaclava go with the kart. A sprint back across the paddock is not the ideal preparation for the race!

Allow yourself plenty of time to find your correct grid position on the dummy grid. Often the dummy grid closes when the previous race goes out. If you are not in position you may well be put to the back of the grid, and everyone else behind your position will gain a place. If you are going to be late because of a problem with your kart, go and stand on your grid spot whilst your crew finish readying your kart. You might be able to butter up the grid marshal for a little while.

Look around to see who is in front and to the side of you. Then, when you assemble on the track for the start, you will know where you are meant to be in relation to the other karts.

If you have any doubt about the procedure for the rolling laps and then the starting system, make sure you ask an official at this stage. Ideally, particularly if you are racing at a circuit for the first time, go and watch the start of one of the earlier races so that you get a feel for the route and the various signals. It is vital to find out where the starting lights are before you get to the grid. Races have been lost before now when drivers have been gazing around still trying to spot the lights when the race starts. The location will vary from track to track. Watching another race start will also confirm the rolling lap and start procedure as each circuit has its own peculiarities.

In the final minutes before the start of the race, allow yourself a few minutes to think and focus on the start and the race ahead. Most races for non-gearbox karts will have a rolling start but if you are on a gearbox kart it will likely be a standing start. Do not start your engine until signalled to do so. Some tracks allow this when the chequered flag goes out for the previous race. When the green flag is waved to signify the start of the green flag lap, be careful to avoid any other pushers as you are leaving the dummy grid. Let the karts ahead of you start to move first and then pull away. Usually, it will take a second or two for the effect of the green flag to work down the grid, particularly if you are towards the back of a full grid.

You will have a rolling lap to warm up and form up. For the first half lap, you can go a little faster, at the speed determined by the pole sitter, and then everyone will be slowed down to get into grid formation. As you go around get a feel for the amount of grip the track is generating. Weaving to warm the tyres is forbidden, so accelerate hard enough to generate some heat by sliding the kart out of the corners a little, but be very careful not to spin. Also warm the brakes up to working temperature, you will want them working well at the first corner. Avoid going onto the edges of the track and picking up the little bits of rubber that have been deposited off the racing line. These are commonly known as marbles and they will stick to your tyres given half a chance.

Then, towards the end of the green flag lap you must reform in grid order, and all slow down for the rolling start. It is the polesitter's responsibility to take the pack round at a suitably slow speed. As the pack slows down you may see some drivers adjusting their carbs in order not to risk oiling up the plug, then setting it for the best acceleration off the line. Do not worry about this until you gain the necessary experience.

If you start from an incorrect grid position, or are adjudged to have started moving from a standing start before the green light, you are likely to attract a five place penalty. This is commonly referred to as a jump start penalty, but in fact it should be termed a false start penalty as the official judges of fact can penalise a driver for starting from the wrong position as well as for anticipating the start.

In a race with a rolling start, you are not permitted to overtake until you have crossed the starting line. Quite often there will be bollards down the middle of the track to deter anyone from doing this.

If the race as a whole is deemed to be a false start, there is a special flag to show this, a green flag with yellow chevron. If you see this, raise your hand to indicate you are slowing and re-form the grid for another attempt. The officials may wave the karts through a short-cut to avoid going round the whole circuit again.

4.7 RACE DRIVING

Good race driving is all about smoothness. You must strive to make seamless transitions from brake to accelerator and back again, and be as smooth as possible with steering inputs. A racing kart is nervous and making sudden movements on the steering or brake will only serve to unsettle the kart.

The components of speed are smoothness, consistency and accuracy. If you master these, your driving will naturally flow. If you try to force the pace, you will be likely to make more errors.

The best advice for the first corner of the race is to be patient, yet alert for anything that may happen. You probably cannot win the race at the first corner, but you can certainly lose it. In your first few races, the main priority should always be to finish, and heroic dives at the first corner are not recommended. You will gain little experience of racing while standing behind the tyre-wall.

Even eight-lap heats are a reasonable length and there is too much at stake to risk banzai first corner moves. Obviously, if an opportunity presents itself and you are decisive and confident, then take it, but measure the risk you may be taking. Most racing accidents happen at the first corner and can be attributed to a combination of cold tyres, cold brakes and, most of all, lukewarm brains!

If you are at the front of the grid with a real chance of winning the race, the first corner can be decisive in the final outcome. If you are further back in the field, self-preservation must be the priority. Try and stay aware of the karts around you, for even if you have taken your sensible pills before the race, some of your rivals may not. There is only one thing more frustrating than taking yourself out of the race at the first corner, and that is being taken out by someone else!

Should you lose a place or two at the first corner, you have another eight laps to try and take them back. Of course, winning is likely to be a distant dream at this stage in your racing career. In your early races, the closest you are likely to get to the race leaders is when they lap you. Do not despair. Legend has it that Damon Hill came close to retiring to the pits and quitting there and then when he made his four-wheeled racing debut.

The safest advice when you are about to be lapped is to keep to your normal line and let the leaders find a way around you. Stories of races being lost by errant backmarkers are legion and if a race leader is taken out by a backmarker, the slower kart will automatically be considered the culprit, whatever the truth of the situation.

Often, the leader will have seen you ahead for a lap or more before he catches you up. That won't always happen, but is quite common. In that situation, he will have seen your line through various corners and will have planned a passing move accordingly. Even if you haven't had anyone behind you in the early part of the race, you should always be ready for the blue flag towards the end of the race. You may be in a race where a number of classes are amalgamated, with some karts much faster than others. If the leader comes past you, be ready for the next few to come soon afterwards.

If your team has timed the fastest kart a quick calculation using the difference in time to your lap times multiplied by the number of laps will show if you are likely to be lapped.

Most leading drivers will prefer the backmarker to stay on his line and maintain the same pace. If the backmarker, with the best of intentions, suddenly lifts off, the leader may be taken by surprise, having planned his move taking into account the relative speed differentials. If you do move out of the leaders way, make a bold signal about which way you are going and be very careful that the leader is on his own.

Many times, an obliging backmarker has pulled out of the leader's way only to find himself in the path of the other kart that was fighting for the lead. Having the race leaders go either side of you can be pretty scary, but that is preferable to moving out of the way of the leader and putting the second-placed kart off the road because you didn't know he was there.

In 100cc two-stroke racing you will notice the experienced drivers dabbing the carb into the corners. They will quickly put their hand over the intake trumpets just as they brake, or indeed as an alternative to braking in a fast corner. The reason for this is to give the two-stroke some extra oil when the throttle is closed. Two-strokes like these depend on the oil in the petrol for lubrication, and if starved may seize. The worst thing you can do is to just ease off the throttle entering a fast corner. It is better to keep on the throttle and brake a little at the same time, whilst maybe dabbing the carb.

4.8 WET WEATHER RACING

There is one certainty about the British climate. During the year it will rain and you will be very lucky to go through a season of racing without having at least one wet race. Most drivers either love or loathe wet-weather racing. Generally, it is seen as a great leveller, giving talented drivers the chance to shine in conditions that may not suit the drivers with the better engines. In extremely wet conditions less-powerful karts can have a distinct advantage as excessive power can simply be an embarrassment on a very wet track.

There is no substitute for experience when it comes to racing in the rain. Invariably, visibility will be poor as plumes of spray are sent up from the karts and in the early laps of the race, drivers in the mid-field can be almost driving blind as they try and peer into a wall of spray kicked up by the leading karts. This can be very nasty, and a cautious approach is demanded, even if you lose time on the leaders as a result.

Various treatments are available to either disperse water on the outside of your visor or prevent misting on the inside. Some drivers just use spit. It can be useful to make a small square of tape to prop open your visor a couple of millimetres, to allow airflow. Other proprietary aids are whirly-visors, a spinning disc that must be fixed outside of your normal visor to spin the water away and provide a clear image.

Just as you would on a slippery road, wet race tracks require a delicate approach, maybe short-shifting in a gearbox kart by using less revs than usual and allowing greater margins for error. Local knowledge of the circuit can be of great importance when the weather gets really bad as puddles can form or water can run across the track in rivers as it drains from the run-off areas. Only experience can warn you about the likelihood of this, and when you race on a track for the first time in the wet, you must be extra-vigilant.

If conditions are so bad that puddles many be forming, try and chat to a more experienced racer while you are on the dummy grid as they may well be able to tell you about notorious sections of the track. Aquaplaning off the track is a scary experience. Local knowledge will also tell you about which corners have a different wet line. Often this is because the usual racing line where rubber has built up is particularly slippy and more grip may be found driving round the outside.

Such are the vagaries of our weather that, on some days, you may find one section of the track dry and the next one wet. If it starts to rain during a race, do not expect the organisers to stop the race unless conditions become very bad. They have a tight timetable and will expect you to cope, at considerably reduced speed. By being careful you can make up many places when all and sundry are sliding off.

Don't forget that if the track has recently dried out from a rainstorm, the grass run-off areas are likely to still be very wet and, therefore, incredibly slippery. Slick tyres don't have much grip on wet tarmac; on wet grass they have no grip whatsoever. The best advice for racing safely in the rain is to extend braking distances and reduce maximum revs through the gears in a gearbox class kart.

You should also pay attention to driver comfort in such conditions. You should put a wet-suit over your race suit as a minimum. If the bottom of the legs flap, tape them round with tank-tape. Some drivers wear domestic rubber gloves over their racing gloves and have spare helmets and boots for the wet. But remember all spare helmets, boots and gloves must have been scrutineered.

On a wet day, dry off the soles of your racing boots as you get into the kart as the last thing you need is your foot slipping off the brake pedal as you dive into the first corner. If you race wearing spectacles, try and spend a few minutes outside before getting onto the kart so that your glasses have a chance to adapt to the ambient temperature. If you have ever walked into a warm pub on a cold night, you will know what a problem this can be. It is bad enough being unable to find your way to the bar, but even more embarrassing if you can't find your way to the correct grid position!

On a day of changing weather, the worst conditions for many drivers, you will see teams on the dummy grid casting anxious glances at the sky. Suddenly, you have a crowd of weather forecasters all trying to decide what the weather is going to do for the next 10 minutes. It is a situation that most drivers hate, as critical decisions have to be made and many races have been won, and lost, on these decisions.

The decision on slicks or wets can be an awful dilemma. Each situation is different, and more experienced drivers will often gamble on slicks if there appears to be a chance of the track drying. However, newcomers would be better advised taking the safe option of staying on wet tyres if the track is less than dry. If you do chose wets on a drying track, reduce the tyre pressures so that the tyres are less likely to overheat.

Often, frantic activity precedes the race as teams make their choices and it can sometimes be a cat-and-mouse affair as rivals wait to see what each other is doing before making a final choice. And, of course, it is not just tyres that may need to be changed at the last minute, as hub positions, chassis stiffness and toe-out is often adjusted to suit the conditions.

An important factor at this stage is to check with the organisers if they are declaring the race dry, open or wet. These are decisions that the Clerk of the Course has to make and communicate to the drivers and can have a big effect on the race. Listen to the tannoy for announcements. Basically, if the CoC has declared a dry race, you can only go out on slicks. It he changes it to an open meeting, it is your choice whether to race on slicks or wets. And if he declares it wet then you must use wet weather tyres, with more than 2mm of tread at the beginning of the race. If the meeting is open then the officials will not wait for you to make a last minute change of tyres on the dummy grid. The grid will depart and you will be left with a kart which may not have its full complement of wheels.

However, in long-circuit racing where speeds are higher, if the race starts on a dry track, the CoC may consider stopping the race if it rains to allow drivers the chance to change tyres.

Finally, if a driver is caught on wet-weather tyres on a dry or drying track, he will find the tyres quickly over-heating. A set of wet tyres can be reduced to rubbish in the course of a few laps on a drying track. In such circumstances, you will often see drivers altering their racing line on the straight to deliberately drive through any remaining wet patches away from the racing line. This is to try and cool the tyres down a little and make them last until the end of the race.

Should you find yourself running wet tyres on a nearly dry track, you really should consider the value of continuing at racing speed against the cost of a new set of wets. They will not last long, and if most of your rivals are on slicks, you are going to plummet down the order anyway!

4.9 SAFETY KART PERIODS AND RACE STOPPAGES

In a long circuit race there are two different types of official car that you may come across on the circuit. Both have specific uses. First is the pace car, which is used to control the field as it leaves the assembly areas and makes its way round the rolling or green flag lap.

A pace car will only be used in conjunction with a rolling start. It is important, during such a start, to hold grid position and only start racing when the lights are switched to green. Being in the right gear at the right time is the key to rolling starts.

Secondly, a safety car is used to control or neutralise a race. This situation will probably develop as a result of an accident that needs to be cleared by the marshals before racing can resume safely. In a safety car period, the car, with lights flashing, will join the track and endeavour to take position immediately ahead of the race leader. All marshals' posts will display a board marked SC and will show a waved yellow flag when the safety car and the following train of karts is in their sector. This will be reverted to a stationary yellow flag when the safety car and following karts move into the next sector. Be wary of getting too close to the kart ahead of you as the queue has a tendency to concertina at various points around the lap. Overtaking is forbidden when behind the safety car, unless you are specifically directed by the observer in the safety car.

When the incident is cleared, the flashing lights on the safety car are turned off and the safety car will peel off into the pits at the end of that lap. When the green flag is waved at the startline, racing can resume. Laps run behind the safety car may or may not be counted as racing laps.

During 1997, a new flag signal was used increasingly to perform a similar function to the safety car. The black and yellow quartered flag can be deployed at all marshals' posts as a way of neutralising the race. When this flag appears, it is the responsibility of the race leader to act as a safety kart and lead the pack around at a non-racing speed.

All the karts in the race should form up behind the leader and follow around in one convoy. Overtaking is again prohibited. This flag is sometimes used on short circuit racing when a medic is checking an injured driver before a decision is made for the necessity of an ambulance, and is a very efficient alternative to red flags and re-started races. When the incident is clear, the green flag at the start line signals that racing can resume. This experimental flag was brought into full use in 1998. All laps run under the black and yellow flag usually count as racing laps, but some clubs add the laps to the race distance. If so, it will be shown in the supplementary regulations.

If a race is red-flagged you must stop racing immediately and raise your hand to warn following drivers. If the red flags are displayed at each marshals' post, then continue slowly to the point where the Clerk of the Course indicated you should stop during drivers briefing. This will often be just before the pit entry lane, to give the organisers the choice of finishing the race if enough laps have been run, re-starting in single file after the accident is cleared up, or sending everyone back to the pits for a new race later on. However if a marshal stands in the middle of the track with the red flag, it means stop safely at that point. Perhaps an injured driver is lying on the track just around the corner.

If less than 25% of the race has been run, a new race will be declared, starting from the original grid positions. If between 25% and 75% then the race will probably be re-started in single file, using the positions from the lap before the red flag. If more than 75% is run, the result will be declared, again using the positions from the previous lap. A single file restart commences with another rolling lap, and no overtaking before the start line when the race restarts by way of the green light coming on. You may have to drive between a set of cones over the start line.

4.10 OVERTAKING AND DEFENDING

The golden rule for overtaking is to be decisive. If you hesitate part-way through an overtaking manoeuvre, either the move will not work or you take the risk of colliding with the kart you are trying to pass. If you are decisive, you should be able to carry out the move.

There are really two different types of overtaking manoeuvre between karts and drivers of similar performance. The planned variety where you build up to it, possibly over a number of laps, and the opportunist move where an error from the driver in front provides you with the opportunity of overtaking.

The planned move can be executed at several different points around the lap. The obvious places are under braking for a corner or under acceleration out of a corner. Outbraking a rival into the corner probably means that you have been chasing them down the preceding straight. Realistically, you will have to at least match the speed of the other kart down the straight and, in itself, that speed may be the product of a faster exit from the corner leading onto the straight, perhaps aided by a slipstreaming effect. Or you might have a more powerful engine which gives you more speed.

Some tracks have long straights with a medium speed corner at the end, lending themselves to slipstreaming and overtaking. However, if you are able to sail past into the corner under braking, the chances are that the other kart will do exactly the same to you on the next lap. This could well be frustrating, but the crowds love a good cat and mouse contest! In this case you need to plan to do the move on the last lap, then defend to the line. If you make the move too soon your rival behind could have the advantage. But beware! Often in this situation another kart follows through and the kart being overtaken finds itself on the outside of a train of karts with nowhere to get back in, and consequently loses many places.

If you plan to outbrake your rival into a corner, be wary of them trying to protect their line. This is the start of one of the most common accidents found in racing, as the leading driver tries to defend the corner as his rival is partly alongside. Frequently the karts will touch and both could spin out of the race.

Ideally, you need to catch your rivals by surprise when making such a move so that by the time they realise what is happening, you are already up alongside them and leaving no chance for them to turn into the corner across the front of your kart. If you can, keep your planned move under wraps until the lap you mean to carry it through.

However, there can be a problem with this. Your move on the inside for the corner is likely to take you into an area of the track you have not previously used. At the very least, on the lap before you mount your bid, take a good look at the track surface for the tighter entry line to the corner. This should alert you to any debris on the track or even any lingering damp patches that could catch you out.

If you have followed your rival for several laps, you should have been able to work out where you have an advantage, as most drivers are reasonably consistent. In this situation, try and not make it obvious where your advantage lies. If you start showing an advantage in certain corners, you are encouraging your rival to defend in the very place where you want to attack. It all comes down to planning ahead.

Many classic outbraking moves start at least one corner before the one where the move is planned. A well-known move is at the end of the pits straight at PF International. If the kart in front is defending at the long right hander, the attacker can take a wide line if not himself being challenged and then get a faster run up the inside to the next hairpin.

You do not need to be ahead, only alongside to claim the corner. It all sounds very easy, of course, and watching an expert execute such a move it can seem very simple. But it is far from easy and can take a lot of mastering. When you do it for the first time, you will be elated!

Overtaking in the middle of a corner is less common, but can be equally as effective. Generally it would be done on the outside line but does entail some risk and, ideally, should only be tried on a driver in whom you have a degree of trust. If you find that the kart in front is consistently moving to the inside under braking to protect the line into the corner, then you could take a more traditional racing line into the corner and carry greater entry speed.

OVERTAKING FOUL

That extra momentum could allow you to go round the outside in the first half of the corner. Then, as you reach the apex of the corner, you are still going past the other kart and have the momentum to carry you out of the corner. If you are fully alongside by the time the karts reach the apex of the corner, your presence will force the rival to maintain a tight line through the corner with a consequent loss of speed.

By taking the outside line into the second half of the corner, you now have the optimum exit line and can make full use of the width of the track as you exit the corner. But beware, some less honest drivers may be tempted to squeeze you out wide on the exit of the corner and you could find yourself up the kerbs and onto the grass. However, most drivers at club level will allow you enough room in a situation like this.

A good example is the entry to the chicane at Shenington. There is a lot of grip on the outside of the right-hander and a brave driver can run round the outside then claim the inside line for the left-hander in the centre of the chicane.

Ideally you must get to know the people you are racing with, and then you will be able to make a judgement about trying such a move. In fact, this knowledge will have a significant bearing on the type of overtaking move you use in the race.

When you make an opportunist move, you may, of course, have already been planning a move when suddenly a chance presents itself and then it is a question of how decisively you act upon that opening. This situation can arise in many different ways. If you are chasing the kart in front, they may be temporarily held up by a backmarker. This could put them off line or cause them to be slow on the exit of a corner; or they have gone off-line going into a corner; or they have missed a gear on the exit of a corner.

On the first lap of a race people often make mistakes when their tyres are still cold and not up to optimum working temperature. This could result in the kart sliding wide in a corner and, quite possibly, the same will happen at the next corner while the driver is still trying to generate heat in the tyres.

If you are alert, you can see this going on in front of you and be ready to capitalise on the opportunity presented. Once you have spotted your opportunity, you need to position your kart in the optimum place on the circuit to ensure a successful pass and counter any prospect of your rival re-challenging. Contrary to what is sometimes displayed at surprisingly high levels of the sport, this does not mean trying to squeeze your rival off the track. There is absolutely no excuse for making contact with another kart when overtaking.

Having been given an opportunity, it is important not to gift it straight back. Consider that just about every driver in a race will make at least one mistake, and probably many more. Even the very best drivers make mistakes, so why should less-experienced drivers expect to do otherwise?

Typically, drivers will make one or two mistakes in the first half of a race and then as the race progresses they will start making regular mistakes, as they become more tired and find it harder to maintain concentration. You may find that if you are patient and can keep lapping consistently, you can win races purely by not making mistakes, rather than by pulling off dramatic and daring passing moves.

You may find that you can dramatically close up on braking, but somehow this does not translate into closing the gap on the following straight. It has been proven on the data-logger that the fastest drivers are those who brake a little earlier but carry more speed through the apex of the corner and hence down the following straight. So turn this to your advantage. Perhaps you have pressurised the driver in front into the corners for a couple of laps. Then try braking a little earlier and carrying the speed through, you may just gain enough to catch the other driver at the next corner.

Putting pressure on the kart in front is a widely-used tactic and can encourage the driver ahead to make the mistake that will present the overtaking opportunity. If you are able to at least match the speed of your rival, there is every chance that, if you were able to get ahead, you could pull away. So, if you are doing the chasing it can be worth positioning your kart at different points on the circuit to make it look as though you are working out where to overtake. Although there are no mirrors to aid the defender, you can often hear the engine note of the approaching kart, and a sixth sense develops to tell you where your attacker lies. As the challenger, if you see the driver in front turning his head to look behind, try and position your kart in his blind spot and he may not realise you are waiting to pounce.

They will then be trying to work out where you have gone and it could be that you are already alongside them. Or, importantly, they start to think that you could be!

When your rival gets to the next corner, they may not be entirely sure just where you are. If this happens, you need to be ready to take full advantage of any gap left by a moment's hesitation. In carrying out such a move, you will have done nothing illegal. You have not deliberately weaved about and neither have you made any contact with the other kart. It is simply a racing tactic that can bring profit.

A useful tip is to study the experts. Grands Prix are not currently noted for overtaking, but pay particular attention to how Formula One drivers set about this very difficult task. It can take many laps of patient planning before the move is pulled off. Try to understand exactly what happened during the overtaking move.

Better still, Champ Car racing does generate overtaking and watching some of the star names work their way through traffic, both on ovals and road courses, can be very enlightening. Watch how an overtaking move is built up over the course of several laps. Their talents are there for everyone to watch, so why not take advantage and learn from the best in the world.

Of course, there will probably be just as many cases where you are the one under pressure from a rival and will need to defend your place without resorting to the type of tactics that will earn you an interview with the Clerk of the Course.

The golden rule, sadly ignored by many who should know better, is not to weave about down the straight. The rules are quite clear about this and the MSA Year Book notes that manoeuvres liable to hinder other drivers such as premature direction changes on the straight, crowding of karts to one side of the track and any other abnormal change of direction will be subject to penalty. Equally, any driver consistently hindering or discouraging the passing attempts of another driver is liable to penalty.

It is a sad fact, however, that far too much weaving goes on, even at amateur levels of racing. If someone has clearly got a quicker kart than you or is simply driving faster, there is no justification for weaving about on the straight to try and block them. Consider that the day will probably come when you are the one being blocked and, doubtless, you will be highly unimpressed by a driver dodging around in front of you.

If you are in front, it is legitimate to take the line of your choice down the straight. However, once you have chosen your line, you should keep to it. If someone is pressing you, it is important to try and sort out where your weaknesses are. If they have a considerable advantage in straightline speed, you are in trouble! In all probability, they will get past you somewhere, no matter how you approach the corners.

Where a series of corners leads onto a straight, you need to concentrate on getting the most out of your equipment through those corners so that you can maximise any advantage you have as you come onto the straight. Generally, if someone is close behind, you should try to go into the preceding corner slower than you would normally, so that you can concentrate on maximising exit speed.

Should you go barrelling into the corner and, as inevitably will happen, start sliding around, anyone sensible behind you will then accelerate through the corner and easily drive past you on the straight. By slowing your kart down carefully into the corner, you will be able to carry exit speed onto the straight. The key is to be hard on the power as early as possible in the corner, whilst not scrubbing speed off on the exit.

Slipstreaming is an art that does have a place in certain classes. The principle is that you use the hole in the air created by the kart ahead of you to gain an advantage in a straightline. By having less wind resistance, your kart may be able to gain a higher straightline speed than normal and be in a position to pull out and pass your rival towards the end of the straight.

4.11 LOSING CONTROL

It is a sure fact that, at some stage during your racing you are going to lose control of the kart. How, when and why will vary, but virtually every incident is the result of either driver error or mechanical failure. The result of losing control can range from a mildly amusing moment to a bone-jarring, wallet-rending shunt.

fovey

LOSING CONTROL

The best way of avoiding too many driver errors is to use test sessions and your early race meetings to build up to your limits gradually, rather than exceeding them and then working back. Of course, many people who start racing want to follow the maximum attack approach, treating every session in the kart as the final round of the World Championship.

In the excitement of the moment, it is all too easy to forget that the purpose of the test session was to run-in a rebuilt engine and not break the lap record on the second lap out of the pits. Self-control is something that some of us only have in a modest amount, but a lack of it could cost you dear in your early career.

The first time you lose control of the kart, and you surely will, it is likely that a fairly harmless spin will be the result. However, even when you finally admit defeat and stop fighting to regain control, you still have work to do. Damage limitation is required urgently. In a gearbox kart grab or press the clutch and keep enough throttle on to keep the engine running. Brake to try and stop the kart going further off than necessary. When nearing the end of the spin, if you are still on the tarmac, try and keep your foot on the brake and not let the kart roll gently. At the same time raise your arm to warn following drivers.

Countless times, karts that have spun then roll slowly into the path of another kart because the spinning driver didn't keep his foot on the brake. Following karts will naturally aim to avoid a near-stationary kart and if it moves another foot or two, there can be disastrous consequences.

However, there is another school of thought for when a kart starts to spin in front of you. At this stage of the incident, the best advice from some experienced racers is to aim for where the kart is at the time it starts to spin, as typically the spinning kart will go either to the left or the right. However, there is no hard evidence to support this, just paddock talk amongst drivers who have been in that situation. In any case karts usually spin to a stop very quickly.

In a non-gearbox kart, if you do not have a clutch, the engine will probably stall. The first priority is to get yourself and the kart to a place of safety. Raise your arm and pull the kart off the track. Then look for a gap in the traffic to try and restart it. If you cannot restart the kart after a couple of attempts pull the kart to a place of safety otherwise the Clerk of the Course will lose patience with you. If you have a clutched engine and the engine is still running do not blast back onto the track. Look for a safe gap in the traffic, raise your arm and rejoin.

If you spin several times during a qualifying session or race, you may also be up before the CoC. It is also quite likely that the MSA Steward will refrain from signing your licence for up-grading from that race. If you do spin more than once, you also need to sit down afterwards and make sure you understand why.

If you are forced off the track onto the grass by another competitor, or find yourself running wide due to an error of your own, you need to do several things to avoid losing control. Don't brake, ease back on the throttle, hold the steering wheel with a very light grip and gently nudge your kart back onto the tarmac, trying to watch where other karts are at the same time.

Arriving backwards on the tarmac while scattering fresh grass cuttings across the track like an out of control lawn-mower will not endear you to your fellow competitors!

At some stage you are probably going to park your pride and joy against the tyre wall. There isn't really any good advice in such a situation, but it is sensible not to brace yourself too hard with your feet and hands as the impact could easily break a wrist that was braced against the steering wheel.

If you are completely unhurt and free to move, raise your hand, get out of the kart calmly and head for safety as quickly as possible, but before you leave your damaged kart, try and check to see that no other karts are heading for you. If you fell off due to oil or a sudden rain shower, the chances are that other karts may make similar mistakes.

If you have any doubts about possible injury or are trapped in the kart, do not panic. Expert assistance will be on hand in seconds and it is at times like this that you will fully appreciate the efforts of the marshals. They will take control of the situation and summon all the necessary back-up to ensure your safe removal from the kart. Put yourself completely in their hands as this is what they are trained for.

The chance of you needing such assistance is pretty rare, but should things go badly wrong, you will be in safe hands. If you are injured or trapped in the kart, you will not be moved until expert medical support is on hand. If there is any concern of neck or back injury, you will be stabilised before being moved. It may seem dramatic, but it is standard procedure.

Even if you have vacated the kart un-aided, you may well be checked by the medical officers. Once again, this is for your own safety. If your helmet is damaged the marshal or the scrutineer will as a matter of course remove the MSA sticker. This is to ensure it is not used again for racing until it has been thoroughly checked over. Helmets are designed to protect for one accident only and will have lost the strength to protect in another. Additionally if there is any possibility of head or neck injury the medics will send your helmet with you to hospital so that the doctors can relate any damage to your injuries.

Fires are thankfully very rare in karting. But if it should happen all marshals' posts are equipped with fire extinguishers. Try and spot the nearest group of marshals and park close to them. By saving them having to run 100 yards with heavy fire extinguishers, you could save considerable damage to your kart.

4.12 AFTER THE CHEQUERED FLAG

Spinning off on the slowing down lap is a sure-fire way of earning the laughter of spectators, marshals and fellow racers. The important thing is to maintain concentration even after you have passed the chequered flag. Be aware of other karts backing off sharply and avoid doing this yourself. In the drama of the final corner, you may have seen the chequered flag, but the rival who is tucked in behind you may not have seen the flag.

If the first they know of the end of the race is when their kart makes sharp contact with the back of yours, it could spoil the day for both of you. So wind the power off steadily and keep a careful watch both ahead and behind for drivers who may not have spotted the flag. If you are on a 100cc two-stroke you should choke the motor to aid lubrication and cooling after the stresses of the race. Do not overtake anyone. If you have just won, the kart in front may be just starting its final lap and will not, unlike you, be planning to enter the pits. Give it room.

As you tour round on the slowing down lap, keep alert as there may be karts about that have been involved in last lap incidents and be trying to restart or make their way to the pits. Sometimes you may want to carry out a check on the mixture by cutting the engine and rolling in. This will allow you to look at the spark plug in the condition it finished racing, not as you trickled up the pit lane and is known as a plug-chop. But do not hold up other drivers by blocking the pit lane.

Remember to keep your crash helmet on until you are stationary back in the paddock. Having slowed down progressively, you will be directed off the track by the marshals. At some circuits, this may be other than into the pit road and you will need to have paid attention at the drivers briefing to find out if you are to return to the paddock by some other route. Normal routine will be for the top six, any other class winners and some competitors chosen at random to be weighed. This is to make sure they and their karts are over the class minimum weight limit. Do not have a drink until the weigh in is finished.

At certain top championship meetings a podium trophy presentation for the top three may take place immediately. You may even be interviewed by the circuit commentator.

However, it is worth remembering that if you are interviewed, the crowd will want to hear from someone who is excited about the race. If you have had a problem with another driver during the race, the podium is not the place to start making accusations. This will only reflect badly on the class of racing, the championship sponsor (if there is one) and any sponsors you may have.

On the slowing down lap, if you are on a gearbox kart with a water temperature gauge, look at it to check the reading. The temperature will typically be at its racing maximum after the rigours of the race and will give you useful data. Try and remember the key values and make a note of them after the race. You may, of course, find that the water temperature is still on the low side against optimum readings and this may lead you to blank off some of the radiator for later heats run in similar ambient temperatures. Once you stop the temperature will rise as the engine loses the cooling effect of the moving air.

As soon as you are back in the paddock after the race, try to arrange for your pit crew to take tyre pressures, but only after any weigh-ins. Adding this to your file of data will help you build experience and help you to judge the correct pressures for the next race.

As you return to the paddock, watch out for officials directing you to scrutineering. At higher profile meetings, the whole field will be directed to *parc ferme*, in other races only selected karts will be directed to post-race scrutineering. *Parc ferme* is a controlled area where karts are held by the officials immediately following the race. Although eligibility checks may only be carried out on selected karts, all karts may be held during this process. Pit crews are not admitted to *parc ferme* and on no account should any work be done on the karts until requested by one of the scrutineers.

Checks may be made to your equipment even after the heats. A cheat may try to use some illegal equipment in the heats, then make the kart fully legal for the final after gaining pole position. Scrutineers will be alert to these tactics and even if they do not strip a suspect engine at this stage they may seal the equipment and demand it is brought to them at the end of the final, regardless of whether it was used again. After the final it is quite usual for more checks to be made, especially after a national championship race. This might only be a check for bore and stroke to check the engines' cubic capacity is within the regulations, or the head volume to check the compression ratio. Or it might be a complete stripdown. Some classes have sealed engines and in these cases you will be asked to produce the logbook so that the scrutineer can check the seal number against that recorded in the book. Usually the first six will have their chassis and engine numbers checked against those put down on the scrutineering kart. Do not remove your kart from *parc ferme* until a scrutineer clearly states you can.

At this stage, drivers will still be pumped up with adrenalin after the race and tempers can easily flare if a driver feels that he has been wronged by another. It is absolutely essential, should you feel that another driver has committed a breach of the rules against you, that you do not seek confrontation after the race. Equally, be cautious of being wound-up by the opinions of your pit crew. They are emotionally involved with your racing and may not have seen the full incident.

If you feel unable to discuss the matter rationally, do not approach the other driver. There is always a danger that, in such highly-charged circumstances, a discussion will lead to physical confrontation. If this happens, the drivers involved face the very real prospect of the immediate loss of their licence and a disciplinary hearing at the MSA. Drivers mounting a physical assault on a rival have been banned from racing for as long as five years.

Your prime course of action is to seek out of the Clerk of the Course and, if necessary, lodge a protest against your rival. However, this should always be seen as a last resort and should be discouraged whenever possible, particularly at club level. In the heat of the moment, your emotions will be running high and it is a good idea to discuss the incident with an independent third-party first of all.

Remember that there are almost certainly two sides to the incident and if it can be resolved with a hand-shake, everyone will go away feeling better about the day. Driver disputes that run from one meeting to the next are not healthy and, after all, this is supposed to be a sport. It may be that a sensible opportunity develops at the next meeting for a calm chat about the incident and it is good to bury the hatchet before taking to the circuit again.

After the race, you will almost certainly want to share the experience with your crew and fellow racers. Tales of heroic moments and ones that got away will abound, and that is all part of the fun of the sport. But it is worth taking a few minutes to note down anything important about the kart's performance for future reference. A quick de-brief with your crew may highlight information and data that will be useful when you next race at that particular circuit.

In the professional classes, a driver will often spend an hour or more locked in the motorhome with his engineer going through a lengthy de-brief and pouring over data. This is not very relevant for the amateur categories, but it is good to sit quietly after the race and make some notes while the race is fresh in your mind. Ask your pit crew about the race; where were the leaders changing gear past the pits? Things like this will be useful information and will help you develop your own driving.

Keep a log with all your data. Testing times, qualifying times, race times - all with a note of weather conditions. Include in the log the number of laps completed and relevant temperatures at the end of the session. This log should also be used to record changes made during test sessions and the results of any changes.

If you have just completed a heat, after about fifteen minutes go and check the results. It is surprising how many drivers do not check and only find they have been missed off the results when they find the grid sheet for the final puts them at the back. Then it is too late to seek amends. But if you find an error within thirty minutes of the results being posted, you can in extreme situations lodge an official appeal. But this should be a last resort. In most cases a simple human error will have been made, and a word with the Clerk of the Course should sort matters out. Results are provisional for thirty minutes or until all protests and consequent appeals have been heard.

Once the kart is safely loaded up and all the equipment packed away, don't forget to collect your licence from race administration and take a note of the final results. If any appeals are pending the results are only provisional. They might not be made final until an appeal is heard at the MSA many weeks later, or until fuel samples have been sent to laboratories and the results obtained. In these cases trophies may be withheld.

Now you will want to stay for prizegiving, normally held about half an hour after the last race. Trophies are usually given out in the ratio of one trophy for every four or five drivers entered in the class. Even if you do not qualify for one of these trophies there are often special prizes for example to the best novice of the day. This may not always be the first novice finishing should that one already be getting another trophy. So it may be worthwhile staying on, and it is good manners to remain and cheer your fellow winning competitors. Think how you would feel if you won and nobody stayed to clap.

Whatever else happens, don't forget to enjoy your racing. After all, that's why you're there, isn't it?

CHAPTER 5
GETTING THE BEST FROM YOUR KART

IN THIS CHAPTER

5.7 AERODYNAMICS

➢ Short and long circuit trim

➢ Wings and downforce

➢ Straightline speed

➢ Front downforce and rear splitter

5.8 INSTRUMENTATION AND DATA-LOGGING

➢ Rev-counters, temperature gauges

➢ What data do you need?

➢ Dash displays

➢ Choosing a system

➢ Lap timers

5.1 KART SET-UP

A kart may look simple but there are an amazing number of potential adjustments. This is why top teams spend days testing, or so they would have you believe. Since there is usually only time for one, or at the most two, adjustments in a typical ten-minute session, the day does go past quickly. To the novice, setting up the kart may seem like a complete black art, but the secret is to test and note down the effect of any changes made and not make more than one change at a time. The aim of this chapter is to cover the possible adjustments and give an idea of the likely effect. Some of the effects mentioned may seem contradictory, but there is a large range of chassis types.

On the chassis, adjustments include front and rear track width, ride-height, front camber and castor, chassis stiffness through torsion bars, seat stays and side-pod bars. Steering ackerman angle, toe-in or out and even the amount of movement at the top mount all affect handling. Seat position and the placing of any ballast are important parameters. Rear axle diameter and type, the number of bearings and the type of hubs used are further variables that can be employed. Tyres are a major variable along with the wheel rim width used. Then there is the gear ratio or ratios, the engine tuning and perhaps the rotary valve or reeds used. On the faster gearbox class karts aerodynamic aids such as the rear wing will need attention.

When you test, try some extremes to feel the effect. This will start you on the way to understanding and reporting on the changes in handling. If you don't notice the difference, the chances are that you need more coaching! With younger juniors the team boss or father must observe the characteristics of the kart from the outside. He or she must learn how changes to the chassis affect the handling and speed without the luxury of driving the kart themselves. Youngsters are not so able to report accurately on the change, but the stopwatch will. While on the subject, it is wise not to over-tire the youngster on a test day preceding a race.

5.2 CHASSIS ADJUSTMENTS

If you push your kart along the ground in a straight line it should roll freely. If it doesn't, then find out what is binding. But as soon as you turn the steering wheel and try to push the kart along, it will be much harder. The reason is that the outside rear wheel must travel a greater distance than the inside rear wheel, but without a differential the wheels must rotate together, so one must skid along as the kart moves. When this effect takes place on the track, especially on slow corners, the kart's forward progress will be impeded. So one of the objectives of setting the kart up is to make the inside rear wheel lift just enough as the kart goes around a corner to prevent this skidding effect.

It can be made to lift by the load transfer from the rear to the front caused by braking and turning actions. Although a kart must not have suspension on a wheel, the flex in the chassis frame itself acts as suspension. Different designs of chassis will demonstrate differing amounts of flex. Addition of torsion bars and tightening of parts like the side-pod bars, the front and rear bumpers and the seat stays will all affect chassis flex.

Before going any further into set-up terminology, it is vital to understand two basic terms. Most of what happens on a race track when a kart starts to slide will be either understeer or oversteer. When you turn into a corner and the front of the kart tries to slide straight on, you have understeer. When the back end of the kart loses adhesion and tries to overtake the front, you have oversteer. This translates as follows. Stiffening the rear will lose grip and increase oversteer, conversely softening the rear will increase grip, reducing oversteer and increasing understeer. The same applies at the front, softening the front will increase oversteer.

These two characteristics have been described in simple terms; understeer is when the front of the kart hits the tyre wall first; oversteer is when the back of the kart hits the tyre wall first!

You must be comfortable in the kart. Find a seat that fits snugly, and certainly is not a loose fit. Manufacturers make a large variety of seats, from basic fibreglass models through to fully upholstered versions some even with variable tension. The flex in the seat can be used to complement the flex in the chassis and change the handling characteristic. For the high speeds found in gearbox classes a high backed seat may add reassurance in preventing whiplash.

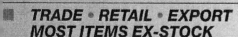

Kart manufacturers should specify the optimum seat position by specifying the distance from the front chassis rail to the front of the seat, and from the axle to the top rear lip of the seat. With the kart on its wheels on level ground, position the seat on some sheets of thin plywood or 100cc/Prokart axle sprockets until it is level with or just below the main longitudinal chassis rails. Sit in the seat and ensure comfort and access to the controls. Your legs should be bent and the pedals must not go over the front bumper rail. The seat should be tilted back a little, you should not be sitting too upright. If possible move the pedals and not the seat to adjust to your height.

Junior karts sometimes have alternative pedal mounts to get the pedals back enough for shorter legs. Mark and drill holes for the top rear seat mounts and put in the bolts, using large plastic washers between the seat and the mounting stay. Check the adjustment and fitting, then put the kart back on a stand and drill and fit to the front mounts. You may need to cut the steering column to get the right reach to the steering wheel with slightly bent arms. Some people have a higher position for the seat in wet weather conditions, but it is easier if you can find a good wet set-up without recourse to moving the seat. A light Junior may need the seat mounted a little higher than normal.

At some point you may have to add lead ballast to bring the kart plus driver up to the class minimum. Generally the ballast should be mounted as low and as central as possible, to keep the centre of gravity low. Put some under the front of the seat, some low down on the side opposite the engine, and some low at the rear. Sometimes in the wet it is advantageous to raise the lead higher and towards the rear. Ensure that all ballast is firmly secured by at least two bolts. No one piece can be heavier than 5kg.

Extra seat stays stiffen the rear end. The stickier the tyre (softer rubber) the more likely is the need for seat stays, or more seat stays. Conversely in the wet seat stays are usually removed or loosened off. But some classes specify the number of seat stays to be used. In prokarts, adjustment of the seat stays may help to make the (heavier) kart ride the bumps better.

Once you are comfortable in the kart the next thing to do is adjust the front and rear track width. For the dry, put the rear wheels wider than the front, perhaps by about 10 to 20 cms. For the wet make the kart square, put the fronts right out and bring the rear hubs in. Record the measurements. Some people measure from the outer side of one tyre to the inner side of the opposite tyre. Others measure the distance from the chassis to a point on the hub or wheel.

It might at this stage be a good idea to check the front corner weights. Obtain a couple of identical bathroom scales, sit in the kart on level ground and place the scales under the front wheels, first checking the tyre pressures are equalised all round. Take the readings. Swap the scales round and re-take the readings. If in any doubt about the flat patch turn the whole kart around and repeat. The corner weights should be within 1kg. If they are not check that the front stub axles are not bent. If this does not correct the problem the chassis must be bent. It is not unusual for the chassis to take a set by constantly racing clockwise, or by hitting kerbs or worse. Take the front wheel off the heavier side and put a large block of wood under the kingpin. Get some heavy mates to stand on the rear of the kart then bounce on the lighter front side until the corner weights are equalised. If significantly out, send the chassis back to the manufacturer to be re-jigged.

Take the kart out and see whether it is basically understeering or oversteering, both into, through and exiting the corners. The aim is to have neutral handling leaving the corner, so as to get the maximum traction without scrubbing off speed by under or oversteer, and achieve the fastest possible speed at the end of the next straight. It is less important whether the kart is under-steering or over-steering on the way in to the corner. However if you need to look after your tyres on a long race the entry characteristic will be more important. You will see some drivers using lots of steering lock on the way in, or throwing the kart sideways on the way in, but the quickest drivers will come out smoothly and be on the throttle earlier than the others. As mentioned earlier, the aim is to get the inside rear wheel to just lift, especially in slow corners. If it does not, the kart will probably bog down and understeer out of the corner.

When testing on the track, use a couple of laps to warm up and get up to speed. Then look for three or four laps to be as consistent as possible. So each session should be for no more than six laps. More than that and you are wearing out the equipment for no benefit. An expert driver will lap within a tenth or two on several consecutive laps, given clear traffic-free laps.

Under and oversteer can be altered by adjusting the track width. Whether this stiffens or softens the suspension depends on the chassis and axle type. Traditionally, and using a kart with a 30mm solid axle, moving the rear wheels in increases grip and hence understeer, or if you are experiencing understeer moving the fronts in will decrease understeer and increase oversteer. So in this case putting the rears out will increase oversteer. But with a modern European style chassis equipped with a 40mm diameter hollow axle (or even 50mm) then the opposite applies. Move the rear wheels out on the axle for more grip, in to lose grip. With the current trend towards wider stiffer chassis this may work even for karts with 30mm axles.

If the kart is understeering through and out of a corner move the fronts out. If it is understeering on initial turn-in, move the fronts in. The handling will be affected by the steering geometry too. Move the wheels at one end, preferably the rear, in or out by 5 or 10mm at a time until the handling is neutral. Then move the fronts and rears equally the same amount out in stages and test to see if it is quicker. Do the same from the datum point moving in instead and test again. By following this procedure you will find the optimum settings for the track on the conditions of that day.

The kart handling will be affected by the amount of rubber being laid on the track by other classes. Mainland European championship racing uses much softer and stickier rubber than we use in most of the UK classes. Their weather is hotter. It is not unknown for a kart to stick to the track on a slow rolling lap, to the extent that a junior cannot then move the kart. In the winter, or for cold weather, the kart may need to be set up narrower all round, with slightly higher tyre pressures, all to generate more heat in the tyres.

With a 40mm or 50mm axle type chassis, adding seat stays will help to keep the back wheels from lifting too high off the ground on cornering. Adding or tightening seat stays, or the rear bumper, or adding a torsion bar will stiffen the chassis and induce over-steer. Some teams will have several different stiffness axle types to try. Even TKM class kart teams might carry three different types of 30mm solid or hollow axles.

Other factors to affect the rear end are the number of bearings and the type of hubs. A two-bearing axle chassis will understeer more than a three-bearing axle type. The wheel hub types can be used to assist in the control of the axle flex. As well as allowing the wheels to be set out wider, large extended hub types will reduce axle flex at the extremities. Some chassis will have removable front cross-members, and clamps between different chassis rails. A significant effect on front to rear stiffness is whether the side pod bars are firmly fixed at both ends or only at one.

With a 250 gearbox three-pedal kart, the difference between the front and rear track width will not need to be so pronounced. Cornering technique is also slightly different, more of a point and squirt by more rolling round the corner then flooring the throttle when the kart is straight. So a wet set-up may not be very much different to dry.

At any track there will be important corners and less important corners. It will not always be possible to get the kart to handle in an optimum fashion at every corner. So set it up for the important corners, usually where there is a long straight following with the consequent overtaking opportunity.

5.3 STEERING GEOMETRY

The other important variables around the suspension are to do with the attitude of the wheels. Initially set the tracking to parallel plus or minus one millimetre. If you stand facing the front of the kart, toe-in is when the leading edges of the wheel rims are closer together than the rear edges. If it looks like both front wheels are pointing out, you have toe-out. Try different settings, probably trying more toe-out first. This might give more bite into the corners and help to lift the inside rear wheel. Castor is not usually adjustable on the more basic karts, but more castor will make for heavier steering and give more of a jacking effect and possibly aid front end grip in the wet.

The castor angle is that at which the kingpins stand in relation to the vertical. The kingpins are the bolts holding the stub axles to the chassis. Changing the castor angle will affect the loading on the steering and you will find the steering get progressively heavier or lighter as you change the castor angle.

The camber of a wheel is the angle at which the wheel sits in relation to the vertical plane. If you are standing at the front of the kart and looking at the front wheels, if the top edge of the wheel rim is nearer the centre of the kart than the bottom edge of the rim, that is negative camber. If the bottom of the rim is nearer the centre of the kart than the top of the rim, that is positive camber.

Most karts will have camber of nearly zero or a small degree of positive or negative. If the camber measures more than a small degree of positive or negative the stub axle shafts are probably bent. If the kart does not have adjustable camber or castor, then it may be permissible to add a camber-kit. This small addition to the front kingpin bolts allows a variation in camber or castor, which may help in the wet. This modification may not be allowed in some classes. Only measure camber or castor with the wheels straight ahead and it should go without saying that it should measure the same each side. Proprietary measurement tools are available. The readings may change with the driver seated in the kart on the ground due to chassis flex. This need not matter; the important thing is to find the settings that make the kart go quicker.

There may be alternative holes on the steering column track rod attachment, or the steering arms. These will adjust the ackerman angle, the amount the inner wheel turns compared with the outer wheel. More ackerman will make the steering heavier, and too much can scrub speed off around the faster corners. It can be used as another aid in picking up the inside rear wheel.

5.4 TYRES AND WHEELS

Tyres are an immensely important part of motor racing and they will be a considerable element of your racing budget. At championship events you will usually choose to buy a new set of slick tyres for each round. Indeed events such as the Super One require everyone to purchase a set of control tyres, so there are no allegations of cheating by using a different tyre compound. But at club meetings you might keep your slicks over several meetings, or purchase slightly used tyres from one of the top championship runners.

A slick tyre works by getting hot. Energy from the circuit and sideways loading heats up the rubber, and the tyre won't really work below 50 degrees centigrade. This is the temperature taken at the point where the tread and the carcass of the tyre meet. That is why tyre technicians push the gauges into the tyre and don't just take the surface temperature.

Surface temperatures are a guide but they aren't enough if you really want to know what is going on. Slicks are designed to carry on working at temperatures up to 110 degrees. At 115 degrees a tyre will be getting to the top end of its tolerance. Over this level, the tyre will overheat and start to fail.

A slick tyre will warm up in a lap or two, depending upon the circuit, the kart, the type of day and how hard the driver tries. A slick tyre will always give you a quick lap when it is new and that should show in up to half a second on the stop watch. The tyre manufacturers will always state that you should condition the tyres by gradually bringing them up to temperature, then leaving them to cool before use, perhaps overnight. Too often the norm in kart racing is to put on a set of new slicks and try and set a qualifying time within a couple of laps. When mounting a new tyre try to put it on the rim without the use of any tools. When seating the tyre into the rim, use a tyre lubricant, remove the tyre valve core and preferably inflate the tyre within a metal tube of the correct diameter. This will keep the tread surface flat and not risk distortion in the centre.

When not in use, take the wheels off the kart and let most of the air out. Over the winter, slick tyres should be stored in a dark, dry area away from electricity and solvents. Tyres should also be kept away from frost if at all possible and kept at a minimum of five degrees centigrade. Some of the compounds can start to fracture if dropped when very cold.

Kart tyres have a large variation in tyre pressures, depending on the type of tyre and the track surface. This is especially true for the SL type of tyre, the harder type. If no-one has suggested a figure start with 20 pounds per square inch all round, but expect to vary from 12 to as much as 40 on some tracks. Stickier tyres need less variation, perhaps in the range eight to 15 in the summer and up to 20 in the winter. In general, higher pressures will generate more sliding and hence more heat in the tyre. Too much heat and the tyre will go off and rapidly lose grip.

Check the hot pressures as soon as you come in from a session, and equalise the pressures. Note the readings when the tyres cool down, to aid setting for the next visit. Then test to find the best front to rear differential. The pressures should rise by two to four pounds from cold to hot. Check that the tyre is being used across the whole width of the tyre. Wheels come in a variety of widths, from the narrower fronts to the widest for the rear. Tyres for the wet are narrower and demand narrower rims. Experiment with different rim widths if possible. Look to see what your competition is using. Check the diameter of each tyre. There should be little variation between tyres on the same axle otherwise power will be sapped by the different attempted rotational speeds.

Changing tyres is something everyone has to learn, unless maybe you are paying to arrive and drive. So take the wheel with the tyre to be replaced, and remove the core from the valve with a special tool to let all the air out. Next you need a bead-breaker or tyre press tool obtainable from most kart traders. If the rim has pegs in it to stop the tyre coming off, then remove the pegs next. Put the rim under the bead-breaker and gradually work around the rim until it has broken clear. Turn the rim over and do the same on the other side. In removing the tyre from the rim, be very careful not to damage the tyre or the rim. Push both sides of the tyre into the well of the rim, then use two small tyre levers on the inner side of the rim to gradually work round the tyre and lift it clear of the rim. Never ever force it. Turn the rim over and without using tools if possible, push the remaining side of the tyre over the inner side of the wheel rim and pull it off. Experts can take the tyre off without any tools other than the bead-breaker.

Clean the rim and remove any rubber deposits. Clean up the threads of the pegs if any. These might either be M5 or M6 capscrews using plumbers tape for a seal, or increasingly new rims come with thumbscrews using a rubber O-ring for a seal. Enter the pegs and screw in until flush with the inner side of the rim, but no more. It might aid tyre fitment to have the new tyre gently warmed up. Push the inner side of the rim into the new tyre and it should slip through. Turn the rim over and with one hand push the fitted side of the tyre into the well of the wheel, tilting the wheel slightly up and away from your body. With a stiff new tyre it might be necessary to 'punch' a V shape in the middle of the tread so the beads go more easily into the well of the wheel. Use your thumbs on the other hand to gently ease the tyre over the rim. It should be possible to do this and completely fit the tyre without the use of any tools.

Next the beads of the tyre have to be popped onto the shoulders of the rim. A little lubricant can be helpful here, some people use Swarfega but others feel lubricant can just make the tyre more likely to come off the rim at an unwanted moment. If you can buy or borrow a former to inflate the tyre into, all the better. These tubular shells prevent the risk of the slick from distension across the contact surface by keeping it flat. Still leaving the valve core out, blow up the tyre only enough to pop the beads onto the rims. Do not over-inflate, and do not point the edges of the rim towards your body in case the rim fails. It is much better to inflate within a cage. After that, fit the cores, screw home any pegs and inflate to the required pressure before use.

5.5 GEARING

Start by gearing for the engine's maximum revs at the end of the longest straight less a couple of teeth on the axle sprocket. Gearing is determined both by the nature of the circuit's corners and the characteristic of the engine. A gearbox class kart should have the axle and engine sprocket chosen to give maximum engine revs consistent with not dropping out of the power band at the end of the straight. It may be possible to change the ratios to suit the circuit, so that it is not necessary to, for instance, have to change gear halfway round a corner. Normally you should change gear at the maximum revs considered safe by your engine builder, which will drop the revs to the place of maximum torque, still in the power band.

A prokart four-stroke will rev out, and not rev much higher no matter how long the straight, so some judgement and testing is required for the correct gearing. It should still be geared for its safe maximum, say 6000rpm, remembering that the engine was designed to be governed to a 3,600 rpm maximum. Correct gearing is one of the most important factors in Enduro racing, where even hundredths of a second per lap add up to many seconds by the end.

A two-stroke 100cc revs on well past the point of maximum power. For instance on a Formula TKM engine, the maximum power point will be about 12,000 rpm. But the maximum revs used will be anything up to 16,000 rpm, because the maximum power is needed coming out of the corners and the overspeed down the straights. A higher formula reed or rotary engine may rev to 20,000 rpm. Testing will determine the sprocket for the fastest lap times. If the axle sprocket starts to get too large or too small, then it is possible to change the engine sprocket. Normally a 100cc two-stroke will be equipped with a 10-tooth sprocket, but alternatives of nine-tooth and 11-tooth can be used. Some tracks can have two ranges of sprockets that both seem to work. At Clay Pigeon either end of a 10-tooth spread can give similar lap times.

The quicker drivers will use less teeth on the rear sprocket. This is because they are smoother and can carry more speed through the corners. It also means they might attain a higher terminal speed, and put less stress on the engine. If you are further down the grid you might add a tooth to give more power out of the corners.

5.6 WET WEATHER RACING

Obviously the slicks are exchanged for wet weather tyres, the newer the better. The rolling diameter will be less, so the gearing may be affected. But so will top speeds, so it may be that the sprocket does not need changing. But you need to check, it's quite possible you will need to add one or two teeth for the wet. Remember your corner speeds will be appreciably less, so to get the same revs on the corner exit will need more teeth on the rear axle. The only disadvantage is that it might cause wheel spin. While slicks are designed to work only when they get hot, wet tyres stop working when they get hot. They have a very different compound to slick tyres and, if the track is starting to dry, the objective is to try and keep the temperature down and you will see drivers going off line to drive through any remaining puddles in this situation. A wet tyre will overheat much more quickly and the blocks of rubber will start to fail.

Other strategies to adopt for the wet include setting more toe-out, perhaps up to eight or 10mm. This will aid turn-in and help to keep heat in the tyres. However it will add to rolling resistance down the straight. Earlier we pointed out how to set the track width to square by setting the fronts right out and bringing the rears in. With a 40mm rear axle type kart it may not be necessary to bring the rears in quite so far. Usually different rear hubs will be used, with less overhang.

Offset front wheels will be used for the wet weather tyres, to push the wheels further out. This means that instead of the wheel bearings being in the centre of the wheel rim, they are offset to the inside. Tyre pressures for the wet weather tyres will be higher, up to 40 pounds per square inch, but less for a heavier gearbox kart, maybe only 20 or 22. As the track dries out the tyre pressures should be reduced to avoid overheating the tyre.

The chassis should be generally softened all round. Seat stays may be removed or loosened. Bumpers may be slackened a little, always taking care that the bumper is still safely secured. Front ride-height may be raised, altering the castor angle and giving better turn-in. If four-wheel brakes, the brake balance needs to be altered to give greater braking at the rear. The aim is to reduce oversteer and make for safer and easier driving. You may find that cadence braking aids deceleration, that is applying the brakes to almost locking up, then taking the pressure off, then repeating. If you lock up the wheels, come off the brakes until control is assumed. Sometimes a different line through certain corners will be quicker than the conventional dry line. This is because rubber is deposited on the normal racing line, which becomes very slippy in the wet.

Finally you may wish to keep the water off the ignition and wiring with a proprietary spray. Be careful not to spray the inside of the plug cap as it can easily pop off during a race. Put a shield in front of the air intakes to keep water out, or use a wet-box to cover them.

5.7 AERODYNAMICS

Aerodynamics is a vast subject that is covered fully in books dedicated to the subject. It is only relevant to gearbox class karts at the faster circuits. It should be noted that these karts can be in short-circuit or long-circuit bodywork trim. The long circuit trim is when an aerodynamic aid such as a large nose cone or rear wing is used. Usually the class weight limit is increased by perhaps 10kg, to compensate for the additional weight of the aids, and try and equalise the performance against those not so equipped.

The basics of aerodynamics are the front nose, acting as a wing, and the rear wings. These are instrumental in deciding how much grip you have at either end of the kart. In simple terms, the steeper the angle that the wing is set at, the more grip it will generate. When you hear drivers talk about putting more wing on, they are, in fact, increasing the angle that the wing is set at so that more downforce, and therefore grip, is generated.

If you look at a Grand Prix car at a circuit like Monaco, you will be able to read the sponsors name on the rear wing very easily. This is because the cars are running a good deal of wing to try and stick the back of the car to the track around the twisty track. If you look at the same car at a high-speed circuit like Hockenheim, the wing will be much closer to flat and the sponsors' name will be much harder to see! In Indycars, when they are running on the very fast super-speedways, the rear wing is completely flat, as any amount of wing will have a detrimental effect on outright speed.

Any wing setting is a compromise between straight-line speed and grip in the corners. You can never have the ultimate of both and every set-up on a racing kart is a balance between those two key factors. You should be prepared to change the settings for every track. However, in the early stages of your learning curve, it can be beneficial to find a set-up that you are comfortable with and stay with it while you learn about the kart.

Also, it is worth remembering that a low downforce set-up with minimal rear wing will make the kart tricky to control in the corners. This is particularly true of a circuit like Thruxton. While the high-speed nature of the circuit calls for low-drag settings, the trade-off is a lack of grip for the corners. An experienced and talented driver may be able to handle this with ease, but a novice could easily be caught out. Therefore, a safe set-up is one with a reasonable amount of wing even if straight-line speed suffers as a result.

It is safe to say that no-one ever crashed due to lack of straight-line speed, but many have come to grief thanks to minimal downforce through the corners! A place or two lost on the straight is far preferable to a high-speed visit to the undergrowth around the sweeping corners.

Traditionally, on the trailing edge of the rear wing is a small flap known as the Gurney flap. This flap dictates the airflow over the top of the wing and leads to an increase in low to medium speed downforce as well as an increase in drag.

The angle and height of the front nosecone will control the amount of grip for the front of the kart. If you increase the wing angle at the front, you are effectively increasing the amount of downforce at the front of the kart. This will give the front of the kart more grip and will also probably make the steering heavier. Normally, this is one way of counteracting understeer, particularly in medium and high-speed corners.

In low-speed corners such as tight chicanes or hairpin bends, the aerodynamics will have little or no effect as you will not be going fast enough to generate much in the way of downforce. If you have problems with understeer in these corners, you will need to look at the mechanical grip generated by the tyres or chassis set-up for the answer rather than the aerodynamics. Ride height can also affect the amount of mechanical grip a car produces.

Some gearbox karts may have diffusers or mini tunnels at the rear. The rule is that nothing must protrude below the main longitudinal chassis rails, except for the obvious brake disc etc. But manufacturers get round this by sweeping up the rear chassis rails to allow the floor tray extension to form a skirt effect and add to downforce. Now on long circuit racing there is sometimes a special class for karts without aerodynamic bodywork to encourage more entries.

5.8 INSTRUMENTATION AND DATA-LOGGING

Nearly all kart drivers will want to have a rev-counter. Only in the Cadet class is this banned, but can be used on test days. Some rev-counters have a maximum revs memory, to aid in gear selection. Usually the connection will be a clip round the high-tension lead to the spark plug.

For water-cooled engines a temperature gauge is a must, to make sure it is not over-heating. In cooler weather it will allow the driver to judge whether he or she can safely blank off part of the radiator. Temperature gauges can also be used for air-cooled engines, either onto the spark plug, and engine head bolt or the exhaust manifold bolt. With practice they can assist in setting the mixture, to run as lean as possible without overheating and seizing the engine.

Data-logging systems used to be the preserve of the well-funded professional teams. However, nowadays, even the most humble club racing kart may be equipped with some form of electronic data gathering system. A data-logging system is a piece of electronic hardware that is installed in your kart and accompanied by analysis software that is installed on a personal computer. In some classes data loggers are not permitted, but you can still use them for test days. Most will require a beacon or at the least a loop under the track. Some tracks have permanent beacons or loops. If you plan to put your own beacon out at the side of the track you must get permission from the Clerk of the Course.

Before you decide to buy a system, see whether the system offers a dashboard and if so try and visualise how that would fit in your particular kart. Look at similar karts equipped with data-logging systems. Each of the systems on the market have a different way of placing information on the display and some may be more suitable to your kart than others. Some have a display that mounts easily on the steering wheel.

The most common information that drivers could have on the display are engine revs, miles per hour, water temperature and lap times. These are typically the basics that you would expect to get from a data-logging system. Not only will you be able to read this information at a glance during the race, but afterwards you can down-load it to a computer, preferably a lap-top, and study the information.

Some systems also include the facility to pre-programme alarm warnings. For instance, if the water temperature rises above a pre-set minimum, a warning light can be displayed. Many also offer a change-gear light, set to come on at a pre-determined rev limit.

DATA LOGGING

Other useful information that will particularly help with finding where you are losing time during a lap will cover things like throttle and brake positions. Of course, if you have such a system, there is no place to hide! But if you are honest with yourself, the data you gain may well highlight exactly where you need to improve to match the class pacesetters. A steering angle sensor will confirm where you are getting oversteer and understeer.

Most of the modern systems are very user-friendly and the supplier will be able to help you get started. Of course, there is always the temptation to get a system because everyone else has got one, so be sure that are going to gain benefit from it before parting with valuable funds.

A very important element, which is often integral, is a lap timer which will give you an instant read-out of the lap you have just completed. More advanced systems can provide a wealth of information from a host of sensors that can be attached to various components.

If full data-logging is beyond your budget or your needs, a simple hot-lap system can be bought. This display links to a transmitter placed on the pit wall to give a read-out of the lap just completed or just picks up a loop buried in the track. At between £100 and £200, the hot-lap system can give you instant access to accurate lap times.

CHAPTER 6
SO YOU NEED A SPONSOR!

IN THIS CHAPTER

6.1 A TWO-WAY BUSINESS DEAL
- ➤ The return
- ➤ Business, not charity
- ➤ Brand awareness

6.2 MAKING THE PITCH
- ➤ Selecting the targets
- ➤ The proposal
- ➤ Selling yourself
- ➤ Non-financial support

6.3 MAKING IT WORK FOR BOTH PARTIES
- ➤ Off-track opportunities
- ➤ At the race meeting
- ➤ Tell it like it is!
- ➤ Sponsor hunters

6.4 KEEPING THEM INTERESTED
- ➤ Team information
- ➤ Press releases
- ➤ Making the announcement
- ➤ When, where and how to announce

6.1 A TWO-WAY BUSINESS DEAL

LOOK — I'LL EXCITE YOU WITH
MY DRIVING IF YOU'LL EXCITE
ME WITH YOUR MONEY.

A TWO-WAY BUSINESS DEAL

Sponsorship. An arrangement where a company gives you an amount of money, you put their stickers on your kart and go off and have a good time. Incredibly, some drivers still see it this way. If this is your view of sponsorship, you are going to fail. A sponsorship deal is a two-way business deal. Nothing more, nothing less.

How do I get sponsorship? That is one of the most common questions that hopeful newcomers ask. To try to shed a little light on the subject, we have included this chapter. But we do not claim to have all the answers and can only provide some pointers and common-sense. To really succeed at sponsor-hunting, you should seek out books that concentrate solely on the subject.

It is a fact of life that many budding drivers cannot afford to compete at the level at which they wish to, simply through lack of finances. Not everyone is fortunate enough to either have family money to spend or a business of their own to fund their sport. If you have either of these, you can probably skip the rest of this chapter and get on with your racing plans.

But those lucky souls are few and far between and most people starting racing will be doing so from their own hard-earned funds. In such a situation, thoughts of sponsorship will undoubtedly surface. But stop and think for a moment. If you cannot even manage your first season of racing from your own resources, are you the manna from heaven that a company with money to spend has been searching for?

I recently received a sponsorship bid from a hopeful youngster. It told me all about his potential, his racing school activities and which championship he was going to win with my money. However, when I dug deeper into the meandering four-page letter, it dawned on me that this chap had not even competed in his first race.

If you are a complete novice, I suggest you forget about sponsorship during your debut season. First, you will probably be so busy that looking after a sponsor will be a demand that you will struggle to meet. Second, how much better it looks if you have some proven pedigree of results to show when you start knocking on doors. Of course, if a sponsor falls into your lap during your first season, don't turn them away!

Before you even start thinking about approaching companies, you must understand a fundamental about sponsorship. It is not charity. It is a business deal. To stand a chance of winning sponsorship from a company, you must be able to demonstrate that the amount of money you are asking them to spend, will be at least matched, and preferably exceeded, by the value you will return to them.

It is not easy to quantify the value of the return, but it must be a central part of your bid. Without it, your proposal is likely to reach the bin within a few seconds of arriving through the letter box. Put yourself in the position of the marketing director at the target company. If the potential value of the return matches or exceeds the cost of the sponsorship, you might just be interested. If the bid is a thinly-disguised request for charity, you will not spend much time reaching a decision.

So how do you go about ensuring that your proposal stands a chance of success? There is, of course, no simple answer to this, but try and look at what a company may want to get from a sponsorship arrangement.

Brand awareness is central to most marketing programmes. A great deal of advertising and a lot of sponsorship is aimed at increasing brand awareness. The company will be seeking to imprint its name and identity into the memories of the audience so that, when a potential customer makes a buying decision, they will think of company X first.

Quantifying the value of this is not easy, but you should be considering several areas where your programme can increase brand awareness. Typically, this can be through TV coverage and media exposure. Your decision about which series to contest may by influenced by potential TV coverage if that is central to your sponsorship deal.

A common reason for sponsorship is of a more philanthropic nature. It is possible that the managing director of a company is a racing enthusiast and sponsors a driver primarily for the opportunity to become involved in the sport. However, these arrangements are relatively rare and often come about due to a personal link between the driver and the sponsor. So, if your favourite uncle has a successful business, make sure you visit him regularly!

The bottom line of any proposal must be that it can deliver benefit to the company that equals or exceeds the value of the sponsorship that you are seeking. If the two amounts do not tally, you are either asking for too much, or giving too little back. Or both!

To coin a well-known expression, you could say that gaining sponsorship is 95% perspiration and 5% inspiration. Those that are good at getting sponsorship will tell you that good homework and determination are essential, and that you just have to keep trying. It's not easy, but why should it be?

6.2 MAKING THE PITCH

We have all heard horror stories of hopeful drivers sending out 500 letters requesting sponsorship and getting three replies that all said no. Using the shot-gun approach of firing at random in the hope of hitting something is most unlikely to reap any rewards and will probably leave you disillusioned.

You have to be more scientific when planning which companies to target. Time spent researching possible targets will save a lot of wasted effort and expense. It is far better to make a bid to 20 likely targets than 500 chosen seemingly at random from the Yellow Pages. But how do you find out who to target?

MAKING A PITCH

First of all, consider the scale of your racing activity and the likely benefits you are going to be able to offer. Grand Prix teams have substantial marketing divisions which are focused on finding multi-million pound targets. Extensive research and forward planning goes into any proposal made and the bid will be very finely tailored to suit the aspirations of the target company.

At your level, it may all seem rather different but you should aim to use the same principals. If you are contesting a club-level championship, you are wasting your time approaching major blue-chip companies. They will be besieged by sponsorship proposals from all types of sports and leisure activity, and unless you have something remarkable about your bid, they will have seen and heard it all before.

Think about the audience that you can deliver a message to. A company specialising in chairlifts for the elderly is unlikely to be very interested in a motorsport programme. However, a company with an obvious interest in attracting a youthful audience (motorsport gets the most attention from males in the 18-40 age range) may be more appropriate.

Consider the geographic area that will interest your target. If the company has a strong local market, you may need to consider how well you can service that need if contesting a national championship. Study your local press, particularly the business pages, and keep an eye out for companies that are expanding or developing new product lines. They may be more interested in your proposal than a company fighting to survive by making staff redundant.

Of course, there is no better way of researching than by tapping up friends and relatives. Most will be employed in some way, and may be able to point you at suitable companies. Look at who is doing the major advertising locally. If they have an advertising budget, they may have something for marketing or the right sponsorship opportunity.

All of these ways, and others, will help you compile a list of likely targets that seem to match what you have to offer. It may take many months to build up your target list but it is worth doing it carefully. Then, your proposal needs to be presented in good time. Don't send out letters in February hoping to find backing for the season that is about to start. Most budgets are set in the autumn and so you should try and time your bid accordingly.

The next stage is to pinpoint the target recipient at the company. Simply addressing your bid to the company is asking for it to find the bin. You need to establish who to send it to, and this will probably be a marketing manager or, in a smaller company, the managing director. Whichever, make sure it is personally addressed.

Ideally, your proposal should be mailed to the appropriate person and then followed up with a telephone call a few days later. This will allow you to check that the bid has reached the correct person, answer any questions and, hopefully, pitch for a meeting for further discussion.

A word of warning. Do not pester any series sponsor for personal sponsorship. The organisers will have done a lot of work to get this sponsor, and will not want them to be constantly bombarded with inquiries from individual competitors.

Another word of warning! Some sponsored championship series have regulations with limitations on the type of sponsorship permitted to competitors. If a major oil company is sponsoring the series, the last thing it will want is to see the leading kart plastered with stickers from one of its marketplace rivals. Also many series have rules requiring decals to be placed on certain parts of the kart, and patches on the overalls. So do your homework and find out about any restrictions first, and how much space will be available on the kart.

That all sounds quite easy, but if your proposal is good enough to get you through the front door of the company, then it has been a success. After that, it is down to you to sell yourself and the concept to the decision-makers.

So what should you include in your proposal? Once again, there is no golden formula for success. But, consider that the average mailshot is only glanced at for a few seconds before being consigned to the bin by a busy manager. If you are to get anywhere, your proposal needs to create an immediate impression and make the reader want to look further. If the first thing that the reader sees is an A4 page crammed full of small print, you are probably doomed.

If you have done your homework properly, you will have identified the corporate colours and identity of the company. With the wide availability of computer drawing packages, why not create a colour impression of your kart and transporter with the company logo already in place? If you cannot do it yourself, you probably know someone who can and even if you have to pay for it to be done, it could just be worth the effort. This stands more chance of grabbing the attention of a marketing manager than pages and pages of prose.

So, that could form the front cover of your bid. You will, of course, need to tailor each copy of your bid to the recipient, but proper research will have produced a small target list anyway. In the following pages of the proposal, you will need some words about you, your kart, your plans and what you expect to provide in return for support.

If you have been recommended to write by a certain person, perhaps a manager or employee of the company, it often helps to say that Mr or Mrs so-and-so recommended I write. Don't underestimate the power of networking. Your corporate or sponsors' guests often find themselves doing good business deals whilst you are out on the track racing.

Don't go on for pages and pages, and don't cram each page full of words. Emphasise the potential benefits available to the company. This should be a very prominent part of the bid. It is questionable as to whether to include figures at this stage. Most experts say not, keep that until you have reached the stage of a meeting.

Keep the initial proposal fairly simple and punchy, something that can be read and digested in less than five minutes. Four or five pages of A4 should be plenty. Your trusty PC should be able to create clean, nicely laid-out pages and the use of photographs is always a good idea.

Make sure the photos are from a bright day, with (ideally) you leading a group of karts, and with spectators in the background. Try and convey the excitement of karting in the photograph. If you cannot find a friend to take a suitable photograph, then use one of the several specialist sports photographers. Their costs are modest and they will have had access to the track for good action pictures. A contact number for Chris Walker, who took the photos on the cover of this book, can be found at the front of the book. Building up a relationship with one of these people will help when you need some pics in a hurry to send to your local paper or sponsor. Another alternative is to have a short video made, but make sure it looks professional.

Include details of how to contact you should they require further information. Ideally, include a daytime telephone number and if you use a number with an answering machine, make sure the message is clean and polite. A sponsor-hunter recently sent out a mailshot to prospective backers inviting them to call a certain number. Had you called that number, the answering machine message went along the lines of: 'Leave a message if you like, we might get back to you but we probably won't'. That's okay if it's only the mother-in-law who is likely to call, but a potential sponsor would probably have hung up there and then.

Should you be lucky enough to be invited to a meeting, your bid now enters a new phase. This is where you really have to sell yourself and many people are not comfortable with this. The best thing to do is to treat this something like a job interview. Get the suit out of the wardrobe, get the oil off your hands and be professional. Don't be too modest about your own abilities and potential, but don't over-sell yourself or your programme either. Be honest and up-beat. Show your enthusiasm for the sport and your own plans.

If you have done your research, you should be able to talk comfortably about the company, its products and any recent changes such as new products or services. Take with you any more background information about the sport including any TV coverage, details of other local companies involved in sponsorship, and so on. There is no substitute to being prepared.

An important opportunity that some people seem to overlook in the quest for money, is to pitch for non-financial support. There are many ways in which backing in terms of parts, facilities and other services can make a useful contribution to your costs while not being a major financial burden to the backer. The fact that you may not be asking for cash support may be far more attractive to a company and, of course, such backers can make excellent subsidiary sponsors for your programme.

You might be able to use the products yourself, such as oil or polish, or maybe the company will be willing to pay for some of your costs through its own ordering system. This could be for tyres, entry fees, printing costs or even the loan of a van for the season.

Should you, after all this, be able to agree backing, you will probably need some form of agreement with the company. A letter of understanding is a recommended minimum in which you spell out exactly what has been agreed and what each party is going to get from the association. It is imperative that there are no misunderstandings at this stage, as they will only become big problems as the season develops. If the amounts of money are substantial, you will probably need to have a formal contract drawn up. If this is so, it is vital to take professional legal advice.

6.3 MAKING IT WORK FOR BOTH PARTIES

In reality, success on the track is not central to a successful sponsorship deal. Obviously, the driver will want to do as well as possible and race wins are good opportunities to promote the sponsor. But a good sponsorship deal will involve much more than just going out and racing at weekends.

Just what goes on around the racing programme to promote the sponsor and its involvement will largely be dictated by the scale of investment and the sponsor's business activities. However, there are a number of things which can be done to benefit the company and start providing the all-important pay-back that the sponsor will want to see.

This list gives some suggestions, but is in no way definitive:

- Use of the kart for displays, conferences, product launches and showroom promotions.
- Use of the driver for company events such as sales conferences.
- Kart on display at company headquarters or in showrooms.
- Use of kart at public events like county shows and exhibitions.
- Use of the racing programme for sales competitions and customer incentives.
- Use of the racing programme for staff competitions and incentives.
- Use of the racing programme in advertising campaigns.
- Customer activity days at kart schools using the racing programme as a focus.

Ask the company for a banner to display above your van or awning. Distribute fliers or brochures about your sponsor and its products or services amongst your fellow competitors.

There are many other ways to link a racing programme to the sponsor's business and these will need to discussed during preliminary meetings.

However, if you can provide some of the above, you will be ahead of the people who simply want to take the money and go racing.

Now, of course, going racing is what it is all about. You may argue that you are a racing driver and need to focus on the racing programme rather than things like the Managing Director's local garden fete. It is true that the needs of the racing must be a priority, but it is the peripheral activities that can really make a difference.

So, what do you do if you are busy trying to run the racing programme and the demands of the sponsor are encroaching increasingly upon your time? The answer depends upon just how much the sponsor is spending. If it is a substantial sum, you are going to need to enlist support, either paid or voluntary, to take on some of the workload to leave you time to meet the sponsor's needs. After all, you probably agreed to them at the start of the deal, so you have a duty to see it through.

If the deal is big enough, you may have to prepare a second, but identical, kart in the sponsor's colours if a busy schedule of showroom displays and exhibitions means that you are not going to be left with enough time to prepare the kart properly and go testing. But, if your deal is modest - and it probably will be - you will need to juggle dates to satisfy both sides of the arrangement.

The next thing to agree with your sponsors is what involvement they want at the race meetings. Once again, this varies tremendously across the sport. At the top level are the bigger-spending sponsors who use each race meeting to entertain guests. At the other extreme are sponsors who just want to come along and get involved at races, perhaps even helping with the kart. Then, there are sponsors who aren't particularly interested in even coming to the races. The important thing is to know what your sponsor wants on race days.

As a minimum, make sure that your sponsor is invited to each meeting and that, if he wishes to attend, arrangements are made for them to gain entry to the meeting as most kart circuits do not offer advance ticket sales. It is also worth making sure they have details of how to find you when they arrive at the circuit. A nice touch is to write to them before each race with these details and an invitation to attend.

Finally, on the subject of finding sponsors, there are some individuals and organisations who will try and secure backing on your behalf. As in any field, some are good, some not so good. If you decide to look at this route, be very clear about what you are going to get and what they are going to keep from any backing they secure for you.

Some young kart drivers amongst us are going to go all the way to Formula 1 and maybe even amass a fortune, albeit having spent one on the way. A talent-spotting sponsor-hunter or driver management agency may want to sign such a driver up for several years. Just be cautious and take legal advice if the deal on a percentage of earnings covers more than a couple of years.

6.4 KEEPING THEM INTERESTED

It is a constant source of amazement that some drivers find sponsorship, go off racing and only make contact with the sponsor when, either the money has run out, or, the time has come to ask for another season's support. If this is how you treat sponsors, do not expect to keep them for very long.

Keeping a sponsor informed about your racing must be an essential part of your planning. If you cannot do it for yourself, then find someone to do it for you, and pay them if you have to. I suggest that, if you have been racing on Sunday, your sponsor should have a fax on his desk at 9am Monday morning telling him about the race. Yes, I know you have to drive home from the circuit in time to get to the pub before closing time, and then get up and go to work on Monday morning. Or if you are a junior, you may have your homework to finish before getting ready for Monday morning school. Don't neglect this either. But if you cannot find the time to keep your sponsor up to date, you will probably lose him.

Your report should be no more than one side of A4 paper, ideally carrying the team name and logo. It should carry basic information about the race meeting, including date, venue and which round of the championship you were contesting. The report should set the scene for the race meeting, detail how the race went and conclude with the date and venue of the next race. Include some quotes from the driver to add some colour, but strictly avoid any dodgy language.

It need not be brilliantly written, but needs to make sense and portray your racing in a positive light. If you have had problems at the meeting, be honest, but don't resort to slagging off your opponents. Try and produce it on a PC that has a spell-check facility so that you can check it before sending it. Also, try and get someone else to read it before you send it, so that they can check that it makes sense. Proof-reading your own work is the best way to miss errors.

If you haven't got a fax machine, seriously consider investing in one. You don't need to have a separate telephone line, just buy a fax that has an in-built switching system so that you plug it into your normal telephone socket. It may also have an in-built answering machine. Once you have one, you will wonder how you ever managed without it.

When you have written your sponsor's report, it is very easy to turn this into a press release that you can fax to your local papers and radio stations. Part of any successful sponsorship programme will be keeping local media interested and informed about the progress of the Bloggs Toiletries Racing Team. A one-page release faxed to them on Monday morning after the latest race is the best way of trying to ensure local exposure for your sponsor.

Look at the paper for its reporting style and write a report for them as if you were one of their reporters, ensuring your sponsor's name is mentioned in not too blatant a fashion. There is nothing a local sports editor likes better than his copy pre-written for him. Keep it short, to the point and try to have a photo in the post to arrive Monday morning, even if it is from an earlier meeting.

Don't forget that your sponsor may have trade magazines for his particular industry that may be able to carry team news. By sending the press release to Toiletries Illustrated you may generate valuable exposure for your sponsor in a publication read by his customers. Equally, your sponsor may wish to have the report faxed to important customers, associate companies or branch offices. Of course, if the list grows you could be very busy on a Sunday evening or Monday morning, and if the project gets too big, look around for professional help.

This same fax list should be used when you first announce the sponsorship deal. However, this may need to be a mailshot as it is best to include photographs from the launch. The press launch is, ideally, the kick-off point for your promotional programme. Normally this will be done sometime before the start of the season and should be planned to generate as much pre-season exposure as possible.

There are many ways of handling a press launch. The Grand Prix teams make it into an art-form but a personal appearance from the Spice Girls may be outside your budget. However, with a little thought, you could come up with a way of getting the picture into the local papers. Try and do something different to the standard photo of the kart outside the sponsor's premises with you grinning inanely while shaking hands with the MD.

The use of a local celebrity in the launch photo will give you a better chance. Why not try the local MP or mayor? They usually love to get their picture in the press for just about any reason, and a successful local business supporting a racing programme should be enough to get them along. You only need them for five minutes to get the photograph taken, perhaps with them sitting in the kart. When you have got the relevant number of prints done, make sure you caption them on the reverse for the benefit of the editors.

Choose the location of the photo shoot carefully. Think about the sponsor's area of business and try and link it to the photo. Outside Bloggs Retail in the High Street on Saturday morning could be a good way of getting a crowd scene, but don't forget to check with the council before you do it!

Aside from the initial press launch and post-event reports, try and spot other opportunities for press releases or sponsor bulletins. Perhaps you have had a particularly successful test day, or carried out some modifications to the kart. By doing this, you should be able to keep the racing programme firmly in the mind of the sponsor, his customers and the local media. And, always send your press releases to the specialist motorsport press. Don't expect too much coverage, but there is no harm in trying. Start it with a short, concise, three-sentence summary that they could use in their Snippets or Round-ups.

Another nice touch for sponsors, and one that need not cost you very much to do, is to present them with a framed photograph of the kart during the season. A good shot of your kart, with the sponsor's name nice and clear, makes an ideal present for the sponsor. Better still, get it framed and then it will probably find its way into the boardroom or reception.

If you are successful with your media campaign, try and get cuttings of any reports of your racing activities and keep them in a presentation file. This is a good record of achievement for your sponsor and could be very useful when you meet to discuss the forthcoming season. Even if your current sponsor does not continue, the file will be a handy tool for discussions with potential alternative backers.

CHAPTER 7
BRITISH KART CATEGORIES

IN THIS CHAPTER

7.1 CADETS (8 TO 12 YEAR OLD)
- ➤ Comer Cadet
- ➤ Honda Cadet

7.2 HONDA FOUR-STROKE CLASSES
- ➤ Honda Cadet
- ➤ Honda Junior
- ➤ Honda Senior

7.3 DIRECT-DRIVE TWO-STROKE CLASSES
- ➤ JICA and variants
- ➤ Formula TKM/Junior TKM
- ➤ Formula Yamaha
- ➤ Formula 100 National
- ➤ Rotax Max 125
- ➤ Formula Rotax Junior UK
- ➤ ICA
- ➤ Formula Libre
- ➤ Formula A

7.4 GEARBOX CLASSES
- ➤ Europa 125
- ➤ National 125
- ➤ 125 Open
- ➤ 210 National
- ➤ 250 National

> 250 International
> Formula E
> Junior Gearbox

7.5 OTHER CLASSES
> Two-stroke
> Four-stroke

7.6 KART CHAMPIONSHIPS
> Super One
> Champions of the Future
> Honda Challenge
> Super 4
> BSA Long Circuit
> British Kart Grand Prix
> Other Championships and Challenges

7.7 SUMMARY OF MAIN KART CLASSES
> The complete list of all main classes for 2002

7.1 CADETS (8 TO 12 YEAR OLDS)

FORMULA CADET (COMER)

Boys and girls can start karting at the age of eight in Formula Cadet and continue in this class until they reach the end of the year of their twelfth birthday. It is a form of karting using specially built mini-karts fitted with 60cc Comer engines. They use a centrifugal clutch and recoil starter. The modification of engines is controlled to keep costs and speeds down and prices are controlled to an agreed maximum. Weight limit for the class is 95kg. There is a series for the MSA Cadet British Championship within the Champions of the Future series.

Engines need blueprinting, or modifying to the limit of the regulations, for the ultimate pace, costing one or two hundred pounds but this is not necessary for the beginner.

Approximate top speed is 50 - 55mph. As with most karts, they are fitted with side pods and a nose cone for safety. Cost £1700 approximately with controlled maximum prices of £960 for the chassis (excluding tyres and fairings) and £399 for the engine. The class uses Dunlop tyres. The number plates are yellow with black numbers.

FORMULA HONDA CADET

The Honda Cadet, with a sealed four-stroke engine is cheaper at around £1500, and a good economic starting point. The two classes may be raced together. It uses one Honda GX-160 four-stroke engine with pull-start and centrifugal clutch and the weight limit is 100kg. An Engine Record Card will come with the engine to show the service history. The normal Honda fuel tank, placed on top of the engine, may be replaced with a remote tank fixed to the kart floortray, in which case an additional fuel pump is also required. The engines have a pull-start. In both cases new chassis homologations have been introduced from the year 2001. The number plates are yellow with red numbers.

7.2 HONDA FOUR-STROKE CLASSES

These classes are run in the Honda Challenge and all use Dunlop tyres.

HONDA CADET
As above

HONDA JUNIOR
A budget class using two Honda GX120 engines. The class is for 11 to 16 year olds with a minimum class weight (kart and driver) of 142kg. Number plates are blue with white numbers. Top speed will be about 60mph. There is a heavyweight option using one GX120 and one GX160 with a weight of 160kg.

HONDA SENIOR
A budget class for both sprint and endurance racing using two Honda GX 160 engines. Starting age is 16 although juniors can move up in the year of their sixteenth birthday. There may also be an MSA British Endurance Kart Championship, a team event for multiple drivers. Weight is 172kg and 187kg for the Heavyweight category where the driver must weight at least 80kg. Prices vary considerably depending on the sophistication of the chassis, from £1700 or so upwards. Top speed will be about 65 to 70mph. Number plates are white with red numbers.

7.3 DIRECT-DRIVE TWO-STROKE CLASSES

Juniors can race in the Senior classes from the year of their 16th birthday

JICA (JUNIOR INTERCONTINENTAL A)
A CIK (European) class for 13 to 16 year olds and the premier junior class of karting. It uses a piston-ported engine with a centrifugal clutch and relatively grippy tyres. A CIK approved 18mm restrictor plate placed between the carburettor and engine serves to limit the maximum power. An external electric starter box is required unless the engine has an on-board starter. This is the Junior MSA British Kart Championship class. Top speed is approximately 75 mph. Cost £2,800 approx. and the engines are surprisingly economic to run. Tyres are Bridgestones, weight limit is 130kg and number plates are yellow with black numbers. Not all

clubs will offer the class, as it primarily races in the national championships. This is not a class for the beginner. There are some regional variants such as Junior Rookie. In this the engine power is also limited by means of an 18mm restrictor plate, tyres are Maxxis, weight is 125kg (135kg for Intermediate, where the driver must weigh a minimum of 62kg, and a 20mm restrictor is used) and it can be raced from age eleven. Number plates are green with white numbers. A senior variant is Formula 100 Piston Port without the restrictor and weight of 150kg using Bridgestone tyres. It has yellow number plates with black numbers and a one inch thick red strip along the bottom of the plates.

FORMULA TKM AND FORMULA JUNIOR TKM

This class is the most popular in the UK and is thus the most common 100cc class to start in. Children from eleven to sixteen and adults above sixteen may race in this economy class of karting. To make racing equal and lower cost, only the TKM BT82 piston port engines may be used. Additionally only British chassis that have been approved are allowed. These homologations can be undertaken every three years and the latest chassis types were introduced in 2001. Earlier chassis are still permitted though. This class is one of the cheapest to start in and possibly has the lowest maintenance costs of the 100cc classes. Retail prices are controlled with the engine at £736 or £835 with the optional centrifugal clutch. Chassis price maximum is £1105 without some of the essential accessories, tyres and fairings.

For juniors, a 19mm Tal-Ko made restrictor plate (20.5mm for Junior Intermediate) must be placed between the carburettor and the engine to limit power. A clutch is optional for easy electric starting and recovery after a spin but then an electric starter box will be required. Cost is £2,000 approximately. Junior weight is 125kg, the Junior Intermediate weight is 135 kg with a minimum driver weight of 62kg and the senior weight is 145kg. A senior heavy or 160 class has the 160kg weight with a minimum driver weight of 80kg. Junior plates are blue with white numbers, Junior Intermediate white with black numbers and seniors red with white numbers. As is usual for the 160/165 variants, a black or white 2.5cm line must be fixed at the base of the numberplates. Tyres for all these classes are Maxxis. Engines are usually blueprinted to obtain the maximum performance within the regulations and this will cost £150 -

£200. A novice would not initially require this to be done. The very equal performance of the karts makes for close exciting racing. Top speeds can be over 70 mph.

The regulations are in the 'Gold Book' or can be obtained from Tal-Ko, Sunderland Road, Sandy, Beds SG19 1QY, the class owner.

FORMULA YAMAHA
An alternative Junior class using the Yamaha piston port KT100 engine. This engine is widely used in kart classes in the USA, Japan and Australia. Zip-Kart introduced the class to offer an alternative to the TKM classes. The weight for juniors is 125kg with yellow number plates and red numbers. The juniors have achieved some popularity in south and middle England but seniors have never caught on. The class is actually arguably the most economic of the 100cc with good wearing Bridgestone tyres and a long lasting engine. Speeds and costs are similar to TKM. The Junior class may be offered in the national championship series and has been a popular choice for Cadets moving up.

FORMULA 100 NATIONAL (PREVIOUSLY KNOWN AS 100C)
A relatively economic class for 16 year olds and upwards only, although existing juniors can move up in the year of their sixteenth birthday. Approved makes of tuned rotary valve engines are used provided the model was introduced/ homologated for 1998 - 2000 or before. These homologated engines will have initially been introduced for Formula A, and the 100 National class offers an extension of life for these engines with the possibility of users buying second hand engines from Formula A exponents. The carburettor can be any butterfly type up to 24mm diameter venturi. Some clubs offer sub-classes for the earlier groups of engines e.g. 100C '95. Certain approved water-cooled engines are permitted in this class and these are very much quieter. Another regional variant is Formula Blue. Tyres are from Vega and the weight is 150kg, or 165kg for the 165 class with driver weight of minimum 80kg. Number plates are green with white numbers. The class will reach nearly 80 mph on some tracks, but more typically 65 - 70 mph.

ROTAX MAX 125
The Rotax Max is a racing pedigree 125cc two-stroke with onboard electric starter and centrifugal clutch. Power output is 28 to 30 bhp so

this class is quite fast and may offer a low-maintenance alternative to 100 National, ICA or Formula A. Becoming very popular. Engines are sealed. Use MGRB slicks and Vega wets. Blue number plates with white numbers and a weight of 160kg.

FORMULA ROTAX JUNIOR UK

This class is a Junior version of the Rotax Max 125, utilising a less powerful engine, still with on-board starter and centrifugal clutch. It is nearly as fast as Junior Intercontinental A, and for that reason is only open to youngsters from age 13, but offers a long life engine and is thus a more economical class. Bridgestone tyres are used, the class weight is140kg and the number plates are red with white numbers. The engines are sealed, and the class is offered in the Super 1 Series, as well as a variant in the Champions of the Future. The cost of an outfit is about £2,450 including tyres. Not all clubs will offer this class until it builds strength of numbers, so check first with your local club before purchase. Not recommended for total beginners.

FORMULA INTERCONTINENTAL A (ICA)

A medium to high cost karting class that is only for seniors. Approved (homologated) makes of tuned reed valve engines may be used fitted with relatively grippy tyres. A 24mm bore homologated butterfly carburettor is used. A CIK-FIA (European) class and the principal stepping stone into European championships from a qualifier championship (where exceptionally 15 year olds are allowed to compete to allow them to go forward to Europe). A CIK homologated chassis must also be used and the rules on modifications and accessories are quite strict. Costs will be up to £3,000. Tyres are from Bridgestone, weight limit is 145kg and speeds will be similar to 100 National. The engines may rev to over 20,000 rpm. Number plates are white with black numbers.

FORMULA LIBRE

With more drivers turning to classes such as Rotax Max, the ABkC decided to formulate a new class for virtually any 100cc 2-stroke engine, giving clubs the chance to amalgamate and increase their grids. Formula Libre runs to the same weight - 150kg - and carburettor rules as 100 National, but uses a Dunlop slick tyre. Any wet tyre from the other ABkC 100cc classes of Formula A, ICA or 100 National can be used, as can number plates from these classes. The class is intended only to run at club level, and no national championships are offered. It is for seniors of 16 years and above, or Juniors transferring in the year of their 16th birthday. It is up to each club whether to offer Libre or the more traditional ICA and 100 National separately. Used equipment can be purchased at very reasonable prices, but engine maintenance costs will however be similar to ICA or 100 National.

FORMULA A

The premier 100cc kart class only for senior drivers using the most advanced equipment; using rotary valve or reed induction homologated engines, large 24mm butterfly carburettors and Dunlop tyres with the most grip. A CIK-FIA (European) class raced in the European championships and as Formula Super A in the World championships. The senior 100cc MSA British Kart Championship series is run within the Elf Hill House Hammond S1 National Kart Championships. Costs will be £3,000 plus and top speed at the fastest tracks can be 85mph. Number plates are yellow with black numbers. Because it is primarily a championship class it will not be offered at most clubs. The weight limit minimum is aligned with Europe at 145kg. At the quickest tracks these karts can reach 85mph. This class will be on the ladder of Formula 1 aspirants and is expensive to compete in due to the short life of the stickier tyres.

7.4 GEARBOX CLASSES

125 classes often use two-pedal karts, based on the 100cc Formula A style but with front brakes, but most 250's and 125's destined to race long circuit will use a longer wheelbase three-pedal type kart chassis. Drivers must be 16 years or over, and 17 or over for long circuit in the 250cc classes. Unless experienced in another branch of motorsport such as motocross, drivers will often choose to start in 125 then may progress to a 250 class. Karts can be purchased second hand for as little as £1,000. A Junior Gearbox class for 13 to 16 year olds using 85cc engines has been introduced, costing around £3,000 with performance comparable to JICA. Races are organised within the Super 4 and at certain tracks.

125 EUROPA

Economy 125cc class using a sealed standard six-speed water-cooled Gilera engine and Italia Motori Birel or approved British made Anderson chassis only for the now obsolete class B. Very quiet and reliable. A new class A is being introduced using a sealed Motori-BAT engine and Topkart chassis. A logbook is issued with each kart and must be carried to show to scrutineers. Tyres are from Continental and weight limit is 180kg, to suit most sizes of driver. Top speed on short circuits is 85mph and just over 100mph on long circuit. Prices are £4500 for the new class A with the on board electric starter. Not all parts of the country offer this class, it is mainly popular in the south and midlands. RPM is the class owner and supplier of the equipment. Owners enjoy a monthly newsletter and participation in a Challenge which includes rounds of the Super 4. Number plates are white with black numbers.

FORMULA NATIONAL 125

A medium cost class using registered 125 water-cooled reed valve engines (or obsolete air-cooled rotary) with a maximum of six gears. The engines have a maximum price limit of £1850, excluding carburettor, engine mount, silencer and exhaust. Prices are therefore from about £3,800 excluding bodywork options. Tyres are from Dunlop. Number plates are blue with white numbers and top speeds will vary from 90 mph short circuit to 120 mph on long circuit using appropriate bodywork. Clubs often amalgamate this class with 125 Open. Weight limits are 180kg short circuit or 185 kg in long circuit trim. In mainland Europe the class runs at 165kg in the European championships and is called Formula ICC with Super ICC for the top drivers having a more open tyre choice.

FORMULA 125 OPEN

This is the fastest 125cc class, using CIK registered engines or engines that have been registered with the MSA for National 125. Most of the CIK engines will be rotary valve, although a few reed induction engines have been registered into the class. The class weight limit at 175kg (short circuit) is slightly lighter than National 125, but the tyres used are the same Dunlops. Number plates are yellow with black numbers and it is a senior class only. Engine power is around 44bhp. A complete new kart and engine is likely to cost some £4,500.

FORMULA 210

A classic class using only the Villiers 197cc engine or clones. Only mainly raced in the 210 Challenge these days. Number plates are red with white numbers and the weight limit is 175kg short circuit, or 185kg long circuit trim with Dunlop tyres.

FORMULA 250 NATIONAL

A class using series production single cylinder 250cc motorcycle engines using piston or reed induction and gearboxes with up to five gears. These are usually motocross engines from Honda, KTM etc and the Rotax 257 in 5-speed form. Tyres are from Maxxis. Tyres may be open in long circuit. Weight limit minimums are 195kg short circuit trim, 200kg long circuit trim. Speeds will be up to 100mph on short circuit and 140mph long circuit. Number plates are white with black numbers. Clubs will often amalgamate 250 National and International. A new kart could cost £6,000 upwards and another £1,000 or more for long circuit bodywork.

250 INTERNATIONAL

A very similar class to the CIK European Intercontinental E with homologated mono cylinder 250cc engines with up to six gears. The most popular engine is the Rotax 257 although TMs and Yamaha are also approved. In addition the engines used in 250 National can be raced in the class with certain restrictions. In long circuit this is the MSA British Kart Championship class. Weights, costs and speeds are as 250 National and number plates are yellow with black numbers, but tyres are an open choice, and many drivers use six inch diameter wheels. The Rotax 257 is often found at lower cost than the motocross engines used in 250 National and spares are also cheaper. There is very little difference in performance on short circuit but the extra gear offers an advantage in long circuit. Power outputs are 60 to 65 bhp. Most of the 250s will race complete with a rear wing. The Rotax engine is no longer manufactured and so the class will become obsolete from 2003.

FORMULA E

The most powerful gearbox class with the ultimate twin-cylinder Rotax or Yamaha 250cc engines producing nearly 80 bhp. Capable of speeds up to 160 mph at the fastest motor racing tracks. This used to be the premier class but costs escalated and the number of participants reduced. Displays green number plates with white numbers and weight is 195kg short circuit, 205kg long circuit. Now raced more at club level within the Super 4 championship with appropriate restrictions on development costs. Still raced to large crowds in France, Belgium and Germany on long circuits with a new European championship proposed for 2002.

JUNIOR GEARBOX

This is a relatively new class to give 13 to 16 year olds a taste of driving a gearbox class kart. The only engines permitted are the TM and Honda 85cc 6-speed. Engine power is about 22bhp, giving the class similar performance to JICA but with much improved stopping power due to the four wheel brakes used. Class weight is currently 155kg. It is offered in the Super 4 national series as well as NKRA and at some clubs. The class will prove especially attractive to those transferring from the likes of junior motocross. Burris slick tyres and Dunlop wet weather tyres are used and the number plates are red with white numbers. The cost of a new machine is likely to be £3,700 but second hand karts could be used to lessen the cost. Most drivers will choose a '2-pedal' kart - throttle and brake - with a hand clutch, but three pedal karts using a foot clutch are also permitted. Like all the gearbox classes the gearchange is sequential, either pushing forward for first, then back for the higher gears or vice-versa.

7.5 OTHER CLASSES

There is a procedure where clubs or associations can put forward new kart classes. Until these are universally recognised and nationally run the regulations for these classes do not appear in the Gold Book. These classes include various engined four-stroke categories.

A couple of manufacturers have offered 250cc four-stroke engines, such as the Ecomoto and Yamaha. These also offer self-starters. They are considerably heavier than the 100cc two-stroke classes. Several traders are promoting four-stroke prokarts with single larger industrial engines from either Honda or similar companies.

7.6 KART CHAMPIONSHIPS

For more information send a large stamped self addressed envelope to the appropriate contact.

TOTAL HILL HOUSE HAMMOND S1 SERIES

Known universally as the Super One, this premier direct-drive championship offers series for both juniors and seniors. Due to its popularity, pre-qualification is often required (Junior, Junior Intermediate and Senior TKM, 100 National, Rotax, Junior Rotax UK, ICA, JICA, Formula A and Cadet) to achieve the 48 entry maximum. Registrations are required by early January, the qualifiers are in March and April then two series run through to October. Each class has six rounds but the MSA British Championship classes of JICA and Formula A have seven rounds. Points are given for all three heats and the final in the other classes but in ICA, JICA and Formula A a system of timed qualifying, two heats and two point-scoring finals is employed. Participants may drop one round, or two of the finals in the case of ICA, JICA and Formula A. The ABkC asks all its member clubs to recognise the numbers of the top fifteen seeded drivers, those that have achieved these positions in the preceding championships. These seeds also do not need to pre-qualify if they wish to compete in the same class in the following year. Offers satellite TV coverage.

Contact Sonja Game, 16, Graham Road, Bicester, Oxon OX26 2HP.

CHAMPIONS OF THE FUTURE

This series won the contract for the MSA British Championship for Comer Cadet. Also runs Junior Yamaha and JICA. It also might require pre-qualification especially in Cadets. It has six rounds including a visit to Northern Ireland. The Cadet seeded numbers 1 - 15 must be honoured as they are the British Championships. It has terrestrial TV coverage.

Contact Pat Connelly, 97, Lower Mickletown, Methley, nr. Leeds, LS26 9JH.

SUPER TWO SERIES INCORPORATING THE HONDA CHALLENGE

Offers a seven-round series for the Honda four-stroke classes, Honda Cadet, Junior and Senior and invited Libre 4-strokes. The top drivers have the right to use their number for the following twelve months.

Contact Roger Abbey-Taylor, 10, Island Close, Staines, Middlesex, TW18 4YZ.

TOTAL HILL HOUSE HAMMOND HIGHLIGHT ABkC SUPER 4

A five to six-round series, for all the main gearbox classes. Guest drivers are able to enter individual rounds if there is space. Top nine in each class National 125, 125 Open, Formula 250E, Junior Gearbox and 250 National have their seeded numbers recognised by all ABkC clubs. From 1998 heats counted for points as well as finals, with the chance of dropping the scores from a set of heats and a final. Europa 125 and 210 combine rounds of the Super 4 within their respective Challenge series for their 'seeded' numbers.

Contact Lesley Allen, Cavalier Cottage, Edgehill, Nr Banbury, Oxon OX15 6DJ.

BSA SUPERKART LONG CIRCUIT

Long circuit championship for National 125, 125 Open, 210 National, 250 National, 250 International and 250E classes. It includes the MSA British Championship for long circuit 250 International. Individual classes, or combined classes, run with car meetings most of the year, and all kart classes come together for two or three all-kart meetings.

Contact Ian Rushforth, 6, Mansfield Avenue, Quorn, Loughborough, Leics LE12 8BD.

BRITISH KART GRAND PRIX

Runs at Pembrey, after many years at its spiritual home of Silverstone. Has classes run to the BSA Superkart regulations for all the gearbox categories.

Contact BARC, Thruxton Circuit, Thruxton, Andover, Hampshire, SP11 8PN.

OTHER CHAMPIONSHIPS AND CHALLENGES

ABkC O Plates: Single weekend national championships for each popular class. The winner has the right to use the O number until the next year's championship. This can give a quick driver, possibly not able to race in the Super One or Super 4, a chance at a universally recognised number. Drivers must be members of an ABkC affiliated club.

Contact Secretary of the ABkC, Graham Smith, Stoneycroft, Godsons Lane, Napton, Southam, Warks., CV47 8LX.

NKRA Championship: A series for many of the 100cc classes, including the Formula Blue etc variants. It has a separate north and south championship which combine for the grand final.

Contact Ron Shone, 125 Lane House Rocks Road, Weymouth, Dorset DT4 9HY.

F1 Northern Gearbox Championship:
A series in the north of England and Scotland for 125 and 250 gearbox classes.

Contact Sue Fairless, 10, Tarn Close, Storth, Milnthorpe, Cumbria.

210 Challenge: A series for the 210 National class, often sharing rounds with the Super 4.

Contact Kate Bateman, 'The Villiers', 36, South Road, Aston Fields, Bromsgrove, Worcs B60 3EL.

Scottish Super Series: Drivers must be a member of the Association of Scottish Kart Clubs.

For details of club championships and winter series, contact the appropriate club secretary.

British Endurance Kart Championship: An enduro series.

Contact MSA for details.

Note: All costs are given excluding VAT.

7.7 SUMMARY OF MAIN KART CLASSES FOR 2002 WITH POPULAR OPTIONS

Class	Number Plate/No	Weight kg Short/bodywork/ BSA	Ages	Tyres Dry#	Wet	Comments
Cadet	Yellow/Black	95	8-12	Dunlop SL3	KT3	60cc Comer engine, recoil starter, clutch
JICA	Yellow/Black	130	13-16	B'stone YEQ**	YEJ	Piston port 100cc, clutch
F.Rotax Junior UK	Red/White	140	13-16	B'stone YEQ	YEJ	Junior version of F.Rotax 125 Max
Junior Rookie	Green/White	125	11-16	Maxxis SLC	WT3	NKRA Junior version of JICA with restrictor
Junior TKM	Blue/White	125	11-16	Maxxis SLC (Green label)	Formula TKM	As TKM with restrictor, economy class
Junior TKM Intermediate	White/Black	135	11-16	Maxxis SLC (Green label)	Formula TKM	20.5mm restrictor, driver must weigh min 62kg
TKM	Red/White	145	16 yr	Maxxis SLC (Green label)	Formula TKM	BT82 piston port engine, optional clutch, economy class
100 National	Green/White	150	16yr	Vega XSL	W2-GB	2000 & earlier rotary valve engines

Class	Number Plate/No	Weight kg Short/bodywork/ BSA	Ages	Tyres Dry#	Wet	Comments
100 National/165	Green/White*	165 (Driver 80+kg)	16yr	Vega XSL	W2-GB	Heavyweight class (driver to weigh min. 80kg)
Formula Blue	Blue/White	150	16yr	Maxxis SLC or HG2	WT3	NKRA listed rotary valve engines
Formula Libre	Any	150	16yr	Dunlop SL4	YEJ, KT6 or W2-GB	Any 100cc engine, any butterfly carb. up to 24mm diameter
Rotax 125 Max	Blue/White	160	16yr	MGRB 'JAG'	Vega W2-'JAG'	125cc direct drive class with clutch and self-starter
Ecomoto	White/red	160	16yr	Maxxis HG3-ECO	WT4-ECO	250cc 4-stroke
ICA	White/Black	145	16yr	B'stone YGB	YEJ	Reed valve, 24mm carb
100 Piston Port	Yellow/Black	150	16yr	B'stone YEQ	YEJ	NKRA senior version of JICA
Junior Yamaha	Yellow/Red	125	11-16	B'stone YEQ	YDK	KT100 engine, clutch

Class	Number Plate/No	Weight kg Short/bodywork/BSA	Ages	Tyres Dry#	Wet	Comments
Formula A	Yellow/Black	145	16yr	Dunlop DBS	KT8-CIK	Latest reed or rotary valve engines
Honda Cadet	Yellow/Red	100	8-12	Dunlop SL3	KT3	GX160 sealed engine, clutch, budget starter class
Honda Junior	Blue/White	142	11-16	Dunlop SL1	KT3	2 x GX120, clutch
Honda Junior Heavyweight	Blue/White*	160	11-16	Dunlop SL1	KT3	1 x GX120, 1 x GX160
Honda Senior	White/Red	172	16yr	Dunlop SL1	KT3	2 x GX160, clutch
125 Europa	White/Black	180	16yr	Cont Sport Club UK	KZ-UK	Class A - Motori BAT Class B Gilera 125cc sealed engine, 6-speed economy class
125 Open	Yellow/Black	175/180	16yr	Dunlop DAH	Dunlop KT6	Mainly Rotary valve, 6-speed

Class	Number Plate/No	Weight kg Short/bodywork/BSA	Ages	Tyres Dry#	Wet	Comments
National 125	Blue/White	180/185	16yr	Dunlop DAH	Dunlop KT6	Reed valve (& air cooled rotary)
Formula 210	Red/White	175/185	16yr	Dunlop SL3	KT5/KT6	Classic Villiers 197 engine or replica
250 National	White/Black	195/200	16+	Maxxis XP5	Maxxis WT4S	Motocross 250cc 5-speed engines
250 International	Yellow/Black	210	16+	Open (6" L/C)	Open	CIK homologated 6-speed
Formula 250E	Green/White	195/205	16+	Open	Open	Twin cylinder 250 plus Rotax 257
Junior Gearbox	Red/White	155	13-16	Burris M15B	Dunlop KT6	85cc 6-speed

Key
* With baseline strip
**Expected to change to YEZ from 01.03.02
+ means 17 years minimum for long circuit
# The approved slick tyres in a class often have a special mark on the sidewall to avoid confusion with similar types of tyres used in other countries.
e.g. Bridgestone will be marked RAC or MSA, Dunlop ABkC or RAC.

CHAPTER 8
APPENDICES

IN THIS CHAPTER

8.1 ARKS-RECOGNISED SCHOOLS
- ➤ The complete list of karting schools
- ➤ Contact telephone numbers

8.2 BRITISH CIRCUITS AND TESTING FACILITIES
- ➤ The complete list of British kart circuits
- ➤ Testing information

8.3 USEFUL ADDRESSES
- ➤ Kart clubs recognised by the MSA
- ➤ Recognised groups
- ➤ Other addresses

8.4 USEFUL PUBLICATIONS
- ➤ Publications and technical papers available from the MSA
- ➤ Magazines and other publications

8.5 FLAG SIGNALS
- ➤ All current flags and their meaning

8.6 GLOSSARY
- ➤ Abbreviations used in this book

8.7 WEB SITES
- ➤ Useful web sites

8.1 ARKS-RECOGNISED SCHOOLS

Aintree Racing Drivers School Ltd
Three Sisters Race Circuit
Bryn Road
Ashton-in-Makerfield
Wigan
Lancs
WN4 4DA

Tel 01942 270230
Fax 01942 270508
Email sales@racing-school.co.uk
http://www.racing-school.co.uk

Tom Brown Racing Drivers School
40 Clydeford Road
Cambuslang
Glasgow
G72 7JF

Tel 0141 641 2553
Fax 0141 641 2553
Email SPORTKART@aol.com
http://www.tombrownracing.co.uk

Combe Karting (Drive-Tech Ltd)
The Bridgestone Building
Castle Combe Circuit
Chippenham
Wilts
SN14 7EX

Tel 01249 782101
Fax 01249 782161
Email info@combe-events.co.uk
http://www.combe-events.co.uk

Deavinsons Kart Centre
Deavinsons Kart Raceway
Rye House Stadium
Rye Road
Hoddesdon
Herts
EN11 OEH

Tel 01992 460895
Fax 01992 468812
http://www.deavinsons.co.uk

Protrain Karting Courses
Unit 6
Hillcrest Way
Buckingham Industrial Park
Buckingham
MK18 1HJ

Tel 01280 814774
Fax 01280 814007
Email protrain@karttraining.co.uk
http://www.karttraining.co.uk

Raceland
Upper Diamond
Gladsmuir
East Lothian
EH33 1EJ

Tel 0131 665 6525
Fax 0131 665 4191
http://www.raceland.co.uk

Lee Rennison Kart School
Clay Pigeon Raceway
Wardon Hill
Dorchester
Dorset
DT2 9PW

Tel 01935 83713

Jim Russell Racing Drivers School UK Ltd
Charnwood House
Forest Road
Loughborough
Leicestershire
LE11 3NP

Tel 01509 219191
Fax 01509 218989
Email sales@jimrussell.co.uk
http://www.jimrussell.co.uk

Sandown Park Kart Circuit
More Lane
Esher
Surrey
KT10 8AN

Tel 01372 471312
Fax 01372 471321
Email info@kartingatsandown.fsnet.co.uk
http://www.kartingatsandown.fsnet.co.uk

Silverstone Drive Karting Centre
Silverstone Circuit
Towcester
Northants
NN12 8TN

Tel 01327 320425
Fax 01327 858268
Email dschool@silverstone-circuit.co.uk
http://www.silverstone-circuit.co.uk

Sisley Kart Racing School
Buckmore Park Kart Circuit
Maidstone Road
Chatham
Kent
ME5 9QG

Tel 01634 201562
Fax 01634 686104
Email sales@buckmore.co.uk
http://www.buckmore.co.uk

SRS Racing Kart School
Podium House
10 The Highway
Great Staughton
Huntingdon
Cambs
PE19 4DA

Tel 01480 860823
Fax 01480 861297
Email sales@srsracing.co.uk
http://www.srsracing.co.uk

INTERNATIONAL SCHOOLS

Go-Karting
PO Box 24250
Dubai
United Arab Emirates

Tel: 00 971 50 651 5945
Fax: 00 971 43 448 232
E-mail gokart@emirates.co.ae
http://www.gokarting.co.ae

AINTREE RACING DRIVERS' SCHOOL LTD

Aintree Racing Drivers' School Ltd at Three Sisters Race Circuit is a founder member of ARKS. We offer a full range of activities to anyone wishing to take up kart racing.

We have arrive-n-drive sessions on Honda Cadets (8-13yrs old), twin-engined Honda Pro-Karts (13 years and up) and high performance Super Pro-Karts which are capable of two stroke lap times (experienced Three Sisters Pro Kart Club members only). We also run open race meetings with Pro-Karts and Super Pro-Karts for hire drivers who wish to turn up and race (telephone for details).

We operate a kart school and we are approved by the MSA to run the Novice Drivers Test (purchase of the MSA Starter Pack is mandatory). We can offer a full three-four hour course which includes tuition, hire of all necessary equipment plus the test (telephone for details). It is also possible to perform the ARKS Test alone (at current MSA prices), however the customer must supply all equipment necessary (karts, helmets, suits etc). Kart schools and ARKS Test are available on most Tuesdays.

Testing facilities are available on predetermined dates for gearbox and non-gearbox karts, for which you will require a current competition licence. Please telephone to check dates and/or pre-book. Three Sisters hosts regular race meetings for most categories of motorsport, spectator and catering facilities are available. Telephone 01942 270230, email sales@racing-school.co.uk or visit our website at www.racing-school.co.uk.

TOM BROWN RACING SCHOOL

Tom Brown Racing Drivers' School has been established since 1980 creating facilities in Scotland to introduce the general public to motorsport.

Karting is one of the many disciplines covered by the school whose facilities have expanded to cover a large area of Scotland and The Isle of Man. Indoor and outdoor centres covering race circuits, The Scottish Skid Control Centre and rally special stages ensure all aspects of driver development are covered.

Tom Brown a past karting and motor racing champion ensures courses run by the school are of the highest standard.

The headquarters of the school are at Sportkart Indoor Karting Centre, Yorkhill Quay, Glasgow. The Centre uses BIZ, ZIP and Sprint karts for drivers from aged eight years and over. Timed practice sessions, birthday parties Grand Prix and endurance racing can all be tailored to suit the individual or group. Expert tuition can take participants from complete novice to obtaining their MSA competition licence with ARKS tests carried out at the West of Scotland Kart Club track Larkhall.

The Racing and Rally Drivers School run Initial and Super Trial Courses, corporate days, race hire and race/rally tuition at East Fortune, (East Lothian), Alford, (Aberdeen), and Jurby, (Isle of Man).

The Scottish Skid Control Centre, Addiewell, (West Lothian) has two 60x 60m floodlit skid pans and an off-road rally special stage. Two and four wheels are catered for with karting, rallying, quad biking, Honda Pilots, 4x4s motocross and road vehicles.

For information on any of the above courses please contact:

Sportkart Indoor Karting	0141 357 5100
Tom Brown Racing Drivers' School	0141 641 2553
Scottish Skid Control Centre	01501 763 763

Email SPORTKART@aol.com or visit our web site at www.tombrownracing.co.uk.

COMBE KARTING

Combe Karting is based at the famous Castle Combe motor racing circuit in north Wiltshire. We have a purpose-built 350m track surfaced in the same SMA asphalt as used at Grand Prix tracks around the world. Practice and training sessions are available for adults and juniors using our 200cc Stratos karts.

Combe Karting runs a junior racing club for drivers between the ages of 10 and 15 years, and the competition is some of the most intense in the southwest. We supply the karts and clothing, and all the drivers have to do is turn up and race. Many of the top drivers subsequently take their ARKS test with the school and move on to race competitively at MSA level.

Adult drivers are catered for in our Public Grands Prix throughout the year when drivers of all abilities do battle on one of the fastest leisure tracks in the area. Again, Combe Karting supplies all equipment and experience gained in these events is a good way of practising race skills before progressing to ARKS training.

ARKS tests are held through the year at weekends if there is no public or private racing. Only four-stroke karts are allowed on our track, but you are welcome to bring your own Pro-Kart or to hire our equipment. All tests are by prior arrangement – at busy times there may be limited availability or specific dates set aside. Contact Max Tyler or Steven Roberts on 01249 783010, email info@combe-events.co.uk or visit our web site at www.combe-events.co.uk.

PROTRAIN RACING PRODUCTS LTD

Protrain was one of the first companies to offer professional training for kart drivers in this country. Protrain Karting Courses were first run in 1982, teaching kart drivers how to improve their driving techniques and kart set-up. The courses and corporate days have developed with time and experience and are now segmented into various areas so that they precisely match a client's requirement.

Karting days

Protrain's Introductory Karting Courses and Corporate days cater for total beginners whilst its ARKS courses and ARKS Tests take drivers to a standard ready for racing. For experienced drivers Protrain offer a range of Techniques Courses teaching race craft, kart set-up and performance enhancements. The courses and corporate days are run daily on a one to one or small group basis using British and European Kart Championship winning driving instructors.

Protrain holds its courses at various circuits throughout the Midlands and South of England visiting different full racing circuits with its course facilities and karts. The whole range of two-stroke karts is used from 60cc cadets through various clutched and direct drive 100cc karts to six speed 125cc gearbox karts. Protrain is a Motor Sports Association recognised kart school and has been deeply involved with the development and operation of the Association of Racing Karts Schools training scheme.

Racing

Protrain also offers race hire for drivers who wish to have the best equipment backed up by professional race guidance and set-up. Protrain is heavily involved with the sale of kart equipment and is the sole importer of the popular 125 Europa class of racing.

Contacts

Gary Chapman or Peter Burden will be pleased to help any enquiries and supply further information either by phone on 01280 814774, email protrain@karttraining.co.uk or visit our web site www.karttraining.co.uk.

RACELAND KART SCHOOL

Raceland is now considered one of the top karting venues in the UK, renowned for its annual 24hr Diamond Endurance Race. With extensive experience in managing karting events, the centre has built up a reputation of professionalism and quality.

Raceland boasts a fully floodlit, MSA-licensed 930 metre outdoor circuit and 250 metre indoor circuit, both of which have been approved for ARKS courses. Other services and facilities at the centre include an MSA affiliated kart club, ARKS school, kart shop, snack bar, classroom, changing room, newly extended paddock, computerised lap timing and weighbridge, and a newly constructed toilet block.

Every conceivable format of karting is run at the centre from corporate events and social/work group bookings to individual practice and racing for beginners and experienced racers alike. Monthly hire kart sprints, junior races, team endurance events, and MSA kart meetings (including 2-stroke and 4-stroke classes) are held at Raceland on the 1st, 2nd, 3rd and 4th Sundays respectively. The circuit also holds regular test days for owner drivers.

Raceland Kart School provides tuition, equipment and advice for anyone looking to obtain their MSA licence. Tuition courses are tailored to the individual's needs, and all equipment can be supplied if necessary. MSA Application Packs are available at reception.

The MSA affiliated Raceland Kart Club organises monthly race meetings for 2-strokes and 4-strokes on the 4th Sunday of each month. Membership costs just £35 per annum.

Raceland is situated 20 minutes from Edinburgh City Centre, 100 yards from the Gladsmuir Junction on the A1 South. For further information visit our Web site at www.raceland.co.uk or contact reception on 0131 665 6525.

LEE RENNISON KART SCHOOL

The Lee Rennison Kart School is situated at the Clay Pigeon Raceway, one of Britain's premier kart circuits. This recently formed ARKS recognised school has been set up to provide karting instruction and courses at the highest level from a- former British Champion. It aims to provide the first step on the ladder to MSA karting, from purchasing and maintaining your equipment, to preparing for your ARKS test and, finally, racing!

We have access to classroom teaching, one-to-one tuition, spectator areas, fully prepared and stocked shop and the facility to hire all the necessary equipment, if required, for your ARKS test. Our equipment is fully race prepared, not de-tuned for the school, so it is the real thing for you to start on.

SILVERSTONE DRIVE KARTING CENTRE

Feel the sensation of speed and wheel-to-wheel racing, only 5cm from the ground at speeds of up to 75mph at one of the world's most evocative motor sport venues – voted British Sporting Venue of the Year 1997 & 1998.

Silverstone Karting offers a huge range of activities from arrive-and-drive sessions through to the ultimate in exclusive corporate entertainment.

Take your choice of either MSA-licensed indoor or outdoor circuits, action-packed GPs or team orientated enduros, junior, single or twin-engined karts, with all events operated by fully qualified professional and friendly staff. All events are available on a full choice of dates, daytime or evening, and with a full selection of catering to suit individuals' budgets.

Enduro events from one and a half to six hours are held on the 1350 metre Stowe Formula 1 test circuit. Karts are supplied and prepared to the highest standards, alternatively we run classes in our events for owner-driver Pro-Karts and Thunderkarts.

For the more serious karter, we can offer ARKS tuition and test courses to get your MSA Kart National B licence, and for the more experienced racer we can offer personalised coaching on a one-to-one basis from our unrivalled team of MSA-licensed instructors.

Karting is great fun and widely recognised as the first rung of the ladder to Grand Prix Stardom, so there really is only one choice – Silverstone, The Home of British Motor Racing. For further details on karting please call 01327 320425.

We also offer other driving experiences for UK driving licence holders, including: single-seaters, race saloons, Lotus Elise sports cars, 4x4, rallying, skid control, E-Type Jaguars, race tuition and corporate days. Activities available at Silverstone, Northants; Croft, North Yorkshire; and Donington, Leicestershire. For further details on Driving Experiences please call 01327 850100, email on dschool@silverstone-circuit.co.uk or visit our web site on www.silverstone-circuit.co.uk.

SISLEY KART RACING SCHOOL

The Sisley Kart Racing School is a founder member of ARKS and is based at the International MSA licensed 1200-metre outdoor Buckmore Park Kart Circuit in Kent. Buckmore Park is acknowledged as one of the UK's most demanding circuits and hosts rounds of all the major 100cc and 4-stroke British Championships. There are full on-site facilities including a clubhouse and kart shop. The circuit is among the most successful corporate karting venues in the UK, catering for 150,000 visitors per annum. The Buckmore Park Kart Club operates from the venue and promotes over 50 events per annum for both owner/driver and hire kart customers.

Bill Sisley has been training young racing drivers for over 25 years and the school still provides tuition very much on a personal one to one basis. The school's graduates include 10 British Kart Champions, as well as Formula One driver, Johnny Herbert, ex-British Touring Car Champion, Tim Harvey and many of today's leading young British single-seater drivers.

Tuition is available for all age groups from Honda Cadets (8 to 11 years old), Junior 100cc TKM (11 to 16 years old), Formula 100cc TKM (16 years plus) and Pro-Karts (16 years plus).

ARKS tests are held on selected dates throughout the year. All tests are by prior arrangement. Gift vouchers are available as well as MSA Kart

Training Packs. For a full colour brochure contact Dawn Wymark on 01634 201562, e-mail on sales@buckmore.co.uk or visit our web site on www.buckmore.co.uk.

SRS RACING KART SCHOOL

SRS Racing was established in 1981 by school principal Stuart Ziemelis. Stuart, a multiple ex-British champion, recognised a need for proper training and a safe introduction for novice drivers into the exciting sport of kart racing. Stuart was also involved with the ARKS Association at its conception and SRS Racing is a founder member.

Activities have now expanded to include both Cadet and Junior confidence building courses, and advanced instruction is available for 100cc Junior and Senior drivers. Most recently the introduction of expert one to one driver coaching has proved very successful.

Once an individual has contacted SRS Racing there are many options open to them. Drivers can attend a pre-ARKS test training lesson, where all the necessary equipment and tuition is provided. The next step is to book and take the ARKS test and once successfully through, the options are to either purchase or hire a kart. Once you become part of the SRS Racing team as either owner or hirer you will receive the complete back-up service allowing the driver to focus purely on racing. SRS Racing has the expertise of an ex-British champion, and the dedication of a first class support team who are all totally committed to providing the ultimate karting experience.

Please telephone us on 01480 860823, email sales@srsracing.co.uk or visit our web site at www.srsracing.co.uk.

INTERNATIONAL SCHOOLS

GO KARTING

Go Karting operates at Dubai Kart Club's Jebel Ali 1KM International Circuit (FIA Category 'C'). Formed in 1998 Go Karting offers full facilities for the first time or seasoned racer. Individual or group instruction at all levels, arrive and drive casual sessions to Grand Prix and Endurance Competitions and our speciality of corporate events our capacity being up to 180 persons per session.

Boasting the largest rental fleet in the Middle East Go Karting has available 20 Honda single engine Pro Karts as well as 10 100cc 2 Stroke National Class. Mini Karts for children and the popular two-seat Thunderkart for training and the occasional joy-passenger.

All equipment is provided. We would recommend those new to the sport come for a pre-ARKS test session. Please contact us for further details by telephoning +971 50 651 5945, e-mail gokart@emirates.co.ae or visit our website at www.gokarting.co.ae.

8.2 BRITISH CIRCUITS AND TESTING FACILITIES

Type	Circuit	Location
X	Banbridge	Co. Down, N. Ireland.
X	Bangor	Co. Down, N. Ireland.
P	Bayford Meadow	Sittingbourne, Kent.
P	Birmingham Wheels	Adventure Park 1 Adderley Road South, Saltley, Birmingham B8 1AD.
P	Bishopscourt	6 miles from Downpatrick, Northern Ireland.
P	Blackbushe	(Surrey) Off A30 at Blackbushe Airport and follow signs towards Sunday Market, OS 175/810595.
P	Boyndie	(Banffshire) 3 miles west of Banff. OS 30/615645.
P	Buckmore Park	Chatham, Kent.
X	Carrickfergus	(Co. Antrim) 91/2 miles north of Belfast.
P	Chasewater	(Staffs) Approx. 1 mile from Brownhills. OS 139/041071.
P	Clay Pigeon	(Dorset) Midway Dorchester-Yeovil on A37.

Type	Circuit	Location
P	Crail Raceway	Fife.
P	Darley Moor	(Derbyshire) 2 miles S of Ashbourne on A515
P	Daytona International	Milton Keynes.
X	Douglas	(Isle of Man).
P	Dunkeswell	(Devon) 5 miles Honiton. OS 192/1307.
T	Ellough	(Suffolk) 2 miles from Beccles. OS 156/447884.
P	Forest Edge	(Dorset) Approx. 4 miles from Christchurch. OS 195 118008.
P	Fulbeck	(Lincs) 8 miles from Newark, off A17 at Brant-Broughton Cross Road. OS 121/909508.
P	Golspie	(Sutherland) Little Ferry, Golspie, Sutherland 82/190030.
T	Hullavington	(Wilts) Off A429 1 mile north of junction 17, M4.
P	Jurby Aerodrome	Jurby, Isle of Man.
P	Kimbolton	(Hunts) 10 miles west-south-west of Huntingdon. OS 153/105696.
P	Larkhall	Hamilton, Strathclyde.
P	Little Rissington (Glos)	RAF Station south of Stow on the Wold. OS 163/206178.
P	Lydd Raceway	(Kent) Near Lydd.
X	Newtownards	(N. Ireland)
P	Nuthampstead	(Herts) 11/2 miles east of Barkway. OS 154/414351.
P	Nutts Corner	(N. Ireland) 4 miles from Crumlin.
X	Peel	(Isle of Man).
P	Pembrey	(Dyfed) 8 miles from Llanelli on A484. OS 159/415036.
P	P.F. International	(Lincs) Stragglethorpe, near Stubton.

183

Type	Circuit	Location
P	Port Richborough	(Kent) Sandwich,.
T	Portrush	(N. Ireland) Car Park, Portrush. OS 1/861405.
P	Raceland	Upper Diamond 5 miles W of Hoddington, E. Lothian on A1.
T	Ronez Loop	(Jersey)
P	Rowrah	(Cumberland) 4 miles from Frizington. OS 82/076186.
P	Rye House	(Herts) Rye Road, Hoddesdon. OS 166/386098.
P	Sandown Racecourse	(Surrey).
P	Shenington	(Oxon) 8 miles from Banbury, off A422 Banbury-Stratford Road. OS 151/359427.
T	St. Athan	(Glam) RAF St Athan, Barry.
P	St. Sampsons	Guernsey, Channel Islands.
P	Three Sisters	(Lancs) Bryn Road, Ashton-in-Makerfield.
P	Tilbury	(Essex) Dunlop Road, Tilbury.
P	Warden Law	11/2 miles off A690, near Houghton le Spring, Sunderland.
P	Whilton Mill	Whilton Locks, off A5 near Daventry, Northants.
P	Wombwell	(Yorks) Dorothy Hyman Stadium, Wombwell, 6 miles from Barnsley. OS 111/403032.

Key: P – permanent track
T – temporary track
X – round-the-houses track

The following circuits are generally available for testing:

Circuit	County	Telephone
Buckmore Park	Kent	01634 201562
Clay Pigeon	Dorset	01935 83713
PF International	Lincolnshire	01636 626424
Rye House	Hertfordshire	01992 460895
Three Sisters	Lancashire	01942 270230
Warden Law	Tyne & Wear	0191 521 4050
Whilton Mill	Northants.	01327 844321

8.3 USEFUL ADDRESSES

KART CLUBS RECOGNISED BY THE MSA

BAYFORD MEADOW KART CLUB
Club Sec: Mr I Ward, Bayford Meadow Kart Circuit, Symmonds Drive, Eurolink Ind. Estate, Sittingbourne, Kent, ME10 3RY; *Tel (w) 01795 410707.*
Comp Sec: Mrs C Ward, Bayford Meadow Kart Circuit, Symmonds Drive, Eurolink Ind. Estate, Sittingbourne, Kent, ME10 3RY; *Tel (w) 01795 410707.*

BECCLES & DISTRICT KART CLUB
Club Sec: Mr R Lock, The Three Hollies, 16 Deepdale, Carlton Colville, NR33 8TU; *Tel (h) 01502 581344.*
Comp Sec: Mrs D Clutten, 11a The Hollies, Norwich Road, Poringland, Norwich, NR14 7QR; *Tel (h) 01508 493822.*

BISHOPSCOURT KART CLUB
Club Sec: Mr D King, 9 Thornhill, Old Newry Road, Co Down, Northern Ireland, BT32 4LT; *Tel (h) 01820 622312.*
Comp Sec: Mr D King, 9 Thornhill, Old Newry Road, Co Down, Northern Ireland, BT32 4LT; *Tel (h) 01820 622312.*

BRITISH AUTOMOBILE RACING CLUB (KART SECTION)
Club Sec: Mr D Carter, Thruxton Circuit, Andover, Hants, SP11 8PN; *Tel (w) 01264 882200.*
Comp Sec: Mr D Wells, c/o BARC Ltd, Thruxton Circuit, Andover, Hants, SP11 8PN; *Tel (w) 01264 882200.*

BRITISH KART CLUB
Club Sec: Alan Burgess, Moorfield House, 15 Moorfield Road, Orpington, Kent, BR6 OXD; *Tel (w) 01689 897123.*
Comp Sec: Alan Burgess, Moorfield House, 15 Moorfield Road, Orpington, Kent, BR6 OXD; *Tel (w) 01689 897123.*

BRITISH RACING DRIVERS CLUB (KART SECTION)
Club Sec: Mr R Lane-Nott, BRDC Silverstone Circuit, Silverstone, Towcester, Northants, NN12 8TN; *Tel (w) 01327 320293.*
Comp Sec: Mrs Sharon Smith, BRDC Silverstone Circuit, Silverstone, Towcester, Northants, NN12 8TN; *Tel (w) 01327 320445.*

BUCKMORE PARK KART CLUB
Club Sec: Mr C Pullman, 38 Bursill Crescent, Ramsgate, Kent, CT12 6HA; *Tel (h) 07778 180352; (w) 01634 201562.*
Comp Sec: Mrs S Rose, Buckmore Park Kart Centre, Buckmore Park Kart Track, Maidstone Rd, Chatham, ME5 9QG; *Tel (h) 01634 201562; Fax 01634 686104.*

CAMBERLEY KART CLUB (BLACKBUSHE)
Club Sec: Mrs J Hall, 8 North Avenue, Heath End, Farnham, Surrey, GU9 0RD; *Tel 01252 721329.*
Comp Sec: Mr T Cope, 13 Fleet Road, Cove, Farnborough, Hants, GU14 9RB. *Tel and fax 01252 540758.*

CARDIFF KART CLUB (PEMBREY)
Club Sec: Mrs D Kilgour, 366 Coed-y-Gores, Llanedeyrn, Cardiff, CF23 9NR; *Tel (h) 029 207 33348.*
Comp Sec: Mrs E Rochester, 2 Golden Brake, Golden Lane, Pembroke, SA71 4BU; *Tel (h) 01646 687078.*

CENTRAL KART CLUB
Club Sec: Ian Rushforth, 6 Mansfield Avenue, Quorn, Loughborough, Leics, LE12 8BD; *Tel (h) 01509 620702; (w) 0116 2324039.*
Comp Sec: Ian Rushforth, 6 Mansfield Avenue, Quorn, Loughborough, Leics, LE12 8BD; *Tel (h) 01509 620702; (w) 0116 2324039.*

CHASEWATER KART RACING CLUB
Club Sec: M Edwards, 109 Beeches Road, Great Barr, Birmingham, B42 2HL; *Tel (h) 0121 358 6541.*

Comp Sec: Maureen Curran, 19 Bronte Drive, Heath Hayes, Cannock, WS11 2GL; *Tel (h) 01543 459013.*

Cheshire Kart Club
Club Sec: Mr L V Jones, 13 Dukes Way, Upton, Chester, CH2 1RF; *Tel (h) 01244 383482; (w) 01244 312696.*
Comp Sec: S A Maybury, 12 Delamere Avenue, Avondale Estate, Buckley, Flintshire, CH7 3BU; *Tel (h) 01244 550561.*

Clay Pigeon Kart Club
Club Sec: Mr S Wojcik, Greylands, Henlade, Taunton, Somerset, TA3 5HU; *Tel (h) 01823 443287.*
Comp Sec: Miss L Marks, 28 North Street, Stoke-sub-Hamdon, Somerset, TA14 6QP; *Tel (h) 01935 822257.*

Coleraine & District Motor Club (Kart Section)
Club Sec: George Harrigan, 30 Laurel Park, Coleraine, Co Londonderry, BT51 3AQ; *Tel (h) 02870 351293.*
Comp Sec: Mr T Hamill, 92 Newmills Road, Ballindreen, Coleraine, Co. Londonderry, BT52 2JD; *Tel 02870 352646.*

Cumbria Kart Racing Club (Rowrah)
Club Sec: Rachel Bewley, Murton Pasture Rd, Rowrah, Frizington, Cumbria, CA26 3XM; *Tel (h) 01946 861355.*
Comp Sec: Mrs Marion Fell, 50 Newton Road, Dalton-In-Furness, Cumbria, LA15 8NF; *Tel (h) 01229 463748.*

Dunkeswell Kart Racing Club
Club Sec: Mrs S Dunn, Carpenters Cottage, Dunkeswell, Honiton, Devon, EX14 4RE; *Tel (h) 01404 891653.*
Comp Sec: Mr R Male, 7 Bell Close, Westbury Sub Mendip, Wells, Somerset, BA5 1ET; *Tel (h) 01749 870858.*

Forest Edge Kart Club
Club Sec: John Crawford, Lilacs, Mount Pleasant, Lymington, Hants, SO41 8LS; *Tel (h) 01590 678409; (w) 01202 294113.*
Comp Sec: Joy Tolhurst, Clapgate Cottage, Newbury Road, Whitchurch, Hants, RG28 7PW; *Tel (h) 01256 893663 plus fax.*

GRAMPIAN KART CLUB (BOYNDIE)
Club Sec: Mr L Aitken, Danesfield, Mortlach, Dufftown, Moray, AB55 4BR; *Tel (h) 01340 820623; (w) 01343 562229.*
Comp Sec: Mrs H M Williams, 43 Chapel Street, Turriff, Aberdeenshire, AB53 3DL; *Tel (h) 01888 563566.*

GUERNSEY KART & MOTOR CLUB (KART SECTION)
Club Sec: Miss Sarah Dempster, Srathmore La Colline Des, Bas Courtils, St Saviours, Guernsey, GY7 9YQ; *Tel (h) 01481 265887.*
Comp Sec: Mrs H Robilliard, Ajamais, 6 Hougue Mague Lane, Capelles, St. Sampsons, Guernsey, Channel Isles, GY2 4WA; *Tel (h) 01481 247892; (w) 01481 247892.*

HODDESDON KART CLUB (RYEHOUSE)
Club Sec: Mrs J Sowden, c/o 33 Kings Place, Buckhurst Hill, Essex, IG9 5EA; *Tel (h) 07944 874128.*
Comp Sec: Alan G Kilbey, 33 Kings Place, Buckhurst Hill, Essex, IG9 5EA; *Tel (h) 020 8281 1141 plus fax; (w) 07944 874123.*

HUNTS KART RACING CLUB (KIMBOLTON)
Club Sec: Mrs Alison Parker, 17 Sandy Close, Wellingborough, Northants, NN8 5AY; *Tel (h) 01933 222239; (w) 01933 276689.*
Comp Sec: Mrs J Wilson, 11 Booth Way, Little Paxton, St Neots, Cambs, PE19 4PU; *Tel (h) 01480 394794.*

ISLE OF MAN KART RACING ASSOCIATION
Club Sec: TBA.
Comp Sec: Mr. W. Kelly, Brookside, Main Road, Kirkmichael, Isle of Man, IM6 1ED; *Tel (h) 01624 878739; (w) 07624 479509.*

JERSEY KART AND MOTOR CLUB
Club Sec: Mr P Troalic, Green Parsley, La Rue Des Buttes, St Mary, Jersey, JE3 3DE; *Tel (h) 01534 483597; (w) 01534 482219 plus fax.*
Comp Sec: Mrs S Davis, 3 Hazeldene Close, La Pouquelaye, St. Helier, Jersey, JE2 3GF; *Tel (h) 01534 872220.*

JERSEY MOTOR CYCLE & LIGHT CAR CLUB (KART SECTION)
Club Sec: Mrs Carol Le Viellez, Sylvian Cottage, Ville Es Renauds, Grouville, Jersey, JE3 9FY; *Tel (h) 01534 852952.*

Comp Sec: Mrs Carol Le Viellez, Sylvian Cottage, Ville Es Renauds, Grouville, Jersey, JE3 9FY; *Tel (h) 01534 852952.*

KENT KART RACING CLUB (LYDD)
Club Sec: Mr C Hilder, 94 Leonard Road, Greatstone, Kent, TN28 8RU; *Tel (h) 07901 670819; (w) 01233 639762.*
Comp Sec: Mr C Hilder, 94 Leonard Road, Greatstone, Kent, TN28 8RU; *Tel (h) 07901 670819; (w) 01233 639762.*

KINGDOM KART CLUB (CRAIL)
Club Sec: John Henderson, Scooniehall Farm, Largo Road, St Andrews, Fife, KY16 8NN; *Tel (h) 07773 260752.*
Comp Sec: Derek Simpson, 2 Chalmers St, Dundee, DD4 7EZ; *Tel (h) 01382 529428; (w) 01382 669384.*

LINCOLNSHIRE KART RACING CLUB (FULBECK)
Club Sec: Debra Sellars, 4 Wydale Rise, Snainton, Scarborough, N.Yorks, YO13 9AG; *Tel 01723 859973.*
Comp Sec: Mrs A Laws, 2 Matfen Place, Fenham, Newcastle On Tyne, NE4 9DN; *Tel (h) 0191 272 2989.*

MANCHESTER & BUXTON KART CLUB (THREE SISTERS, BRYN ROAD, ASHTON-IN-MAKERFIELD, LANCS.; TEL 01942 270230).
Club Sec: Kath Bott, Launswood, Wigan Road, Shevington, Wigan, WN6 8LY; *Tel (h) 01257 252722; (w) 01257 253742.*
Comp Sec: Kath Bott, Launswood, Wigan Road, Shevington, Wigan, WN6 8LY; *Tel (h) 01257 252722; (w) 01257 253742.*

NATIONAL ASSOCIATION FOR SCHOOL & YOUTH GROUP KARTING
Club Sec: Mr S Badcock, 37 Knightscliffe Way, Northampton, NN5 6DF; *Tel 01604 587915; (w) 01536 513165.*
Comp Sec: Keith Fletcher, 2 Ainsdale Close, Buckley, Clwyd, CH7 2NE.

NORTH OF SCOTLAND KART CLUB (GOLSPIE)
Club Sec: Mr J W Archer, 3 Obsdale Park, Alness, Ross-Shire, IV17 0TP; *Tel (h) 01349 884036.*
Comp Sec: David MacDonald, 20 Seaforth Road, Golspie, Sutherland, KW10 6TJ; *Tel (h) 01408 633282.*

RACELAND KART CLUB
Club Sec: Fergus Laird, Upper Diamond, Gladsmuir, East Lothian, EH33 1EJ; *(w) 0131 665 6625.*
Comp Sec: Fergus Laird, Upper Diamond, Gladsmuir, East Lothian, EH33 1EJ; *(w) 0131 665 6625.*

RISSINGTON KART CLUB (LITTLE RISSINGTON RAF STATION)
Club Sec: Mike Chalmers, 40 Dulnan Close, Tilehurst, Reading RG30 4YW. *(h) 0118 942 5535; (w) 0118 983 7477.*
Comp Sec: Mrs J Dredge, 4 Goodwood Close, Burghfield Common, Reading, RG7 3EZ; *Tel & fax (h) 01189 836070.*

ROCHESTER MOTOR CLUB (KART SECTION)
Club Sec: R D McCabe, 5 Old Loose Close, Loose, Maidstone, Kent, ME15 0BJ; *Tel (h) 01622 745714; (m) 07976 275079.*
Comp Sec: R Sheffield, 103 Tudor Avenue, Worcester Park, Surrey, KT4 8TU; *Tel (h) 020 8330 5810; (m) 07710 288074.*

ROTAX MAX OWNERS CLUB
Club Sec: Mrs C Rennison, Rose Cottage, Kingcombe Road, Hooke, Beaminster, Dorset, DT8 3PD; *Tel (h) 01306 863753; (w) 01935 83713.*
Comp Sec: Mrs C Rennison, Rose Cottage, Kingcombe Road, Hooke, Beaminster, Dorset, DT8 3PD; *Tel (h) 01306 863753; (w) 01935 83713.*

SANDOWN PARK KART CLUB
Club Sec: Marilyn Rivalland, C/OSandown Park, More Lane, Esher, Surrey, KT10 8AN; *Tel (w) 01372 471312; fax 01372 471308.*
Comp Sec: Marilyn Rivalland, Sandown Park, More Lane, Esher, Surrey, KT10 8AN; *Tel (w) 01372 471312; fax 01372 471308.*

SHENINGTON KART RACING CLUB
Club Sec: G M Smith, Stoneycroft, Godsons Lane, Napton, Southam, Warwickshire, CV47 8LX; *Tel (h) 01926 812177 plus fax.*
Comp Sec: S G Game, 16 Graham Rd, Bicester, Oxon, OX26 2HP; *Tel (h) 01869 320157; Fax 01869 247981. www.sheningtonkrc.co.uk*

SILVERSTONE RACING CLUB (KART SECTION)
Club Sec: J Garton, Silverstone Circuit, Silverstone, Towcester, Northants, NN12 8TN; *Tel (w) 01327 320 267.*

Comp Sec: Mr J Howkins, Silverstone Circuit, Silverstone, Towcester, Northants, NN12 8TN; *Tel (w) 01327 320379.*

SOUTH YORKSHIRE KART CLUB (WOMBWELL)
Club Sec: Mrs Patricia Lord, 9 Fern Close, Springhead, Oldham, OL4 4NS; *Tel (h) 0161 633 4519 plus fax; (w) 0161 633 4519.*
Comp Sec: Valerie Lord, 58 Hyde Road, Mottram, Hyde, SK14 6NG; *Tel (h) 01457 764441.*

ST ATHAN KART RACING CLUB (LLANDOW)
Club Sec: P Jones, 28 Fairfield Road, Bridgend, CF31 3DU; *Tel 07760 154640.*
Comp Sec: Mrs D Keatley, 134 Fidlas Road, Llanishen, Cardiff, CF14 0NE; *Tel (h) 029 2076 3332.*

TRENT VALLEY KART CLUB (PF INTERNATIONAL)
Club Sec: Mr J Connelly, 37 Lower Mickletown, Methley, Leeds, West Yorkshire, LS26 9JH; *Tel (h) 01977 515204; Fax 01977 516839.*
Comp Sec: Mrs Patricia Connelly, 37 Lower Mickletown, Methley, Leeds, West Yorkshire, LS26 9JH; *Tel (h) 01977 515204; Fax 01977 516839.*

TWO COUNTIES KART CLUB (HULLAVINGTON)
Club Sec: Bruce Taylor, 11 Westdowne Close, Weymouth, Dorset, DT4 0RW; *Tel (h) 01305 773680.*
Comp Sec: Julie Shone, 125 Lanehouse Rocks Rd, Weymouth, Dorset, DT4 9HY; *Tel (h) 01305 774074.*

ULSTER KART CLUB (NUTTS CORNER)
Club Sec: Mrs Rae Curran, 7 Castle Is Dr, Rosevale, Newtownards, Co Down, N Ireland, BT23 7BU; *(w) 02891 822187; Fax 02891 819724.*
Comp Sec: Mr G Magennis, 9 Steedstown Road, Lisburn, Co. Antrim, BT28 3XS; *Tel 02892 648567.*

WARDEN LAW KART CLUB
Club + Comp Sec: Anne Laws, 2 Matfen Place, Newcastle Upon Tyne, NE4 9DN; *Tel (h) 0191 273 0830.*

WEST OF SCOTLAND KART CLUB
Club Sec: Mr Bill McDonald, 51 Newton Road, Lenzie, Glasgow, G66 5LS; *Tel (h) 0141 775 1506.*
Comp Sec: Mrs Ina Nelson, 20 Glenside Gardens, Armadale, West Lothian, Scotland, EH48 3RA; *Tel (h) 01501 731870.*

WHILTON MILL KART CLUB
Club Sec: Peter Eyton-Jones, Whilton Mill, Whilton Locks, Daventry, Northants., NN11 5NH; *Tel 01327 843822.*
Comp Sec: Rita Chapman, 23 Foxglove Close, Castle Meadow, Buckingham, MK18 1FU; *Tel (h) 01280 816512; (w) 01280 816512.*

RECOGNISED GROUPS

Association of British Kart Clubs
Secretary: G M Smith, Stoneycroft, Godsons Lane, Napton, Southam, Warwicks, CV47 8LX. *Tel (h) 01926 812177.* E-mail: *graham@abkc.org.uk; Website: www.abkc.org.uk*
Member Clubs: Bayford Meadow KC - Beccles & District KC - Buckmore Park KC - Camberley KC - Cardiff KC - Chasewater KC - Clay Pigeon KC - Cumbria KC - Dunkeswell KC - Forest Edge KC - Grampian KC - Guernsey Kart & Motor Club - Hunts KC - Kent KRC - Kingdom KC - Lincs KC - Manchester & Buxton KC - North of Scotland KC - Raceland KC - Rissington KC - Rotax Max Owners Club - St. Athan KC - Sandown Park KC - Shenington KRC - South Yorks KC - Trent Valley KC - Ulster KC - Warden Law KC - West of Scotland KC - Whilton Mill KC.

Association of Scottish Kart Clubs
Secretary: TBA.

British Superkart Association
Secretary: Mr I Rushforth, 6 Mansfield Avenue, Quorn, Loughborough, LE12 8BD. *Tel (h) 01509 620702.*

National Four Stroke Kart Racing Association
Secretary: Mr Kelvin Nichols, 2F Wiggall Road, Lee, London, SE12 8HE. *Tel (h) 020 8318 6039 (b) 0973 176806.*

National Kart Racing Association
Secretary: Mrs J Shone, 125 Lane House Rocks Road, Weymouth, Dorset DT4 9HY. *Tel (h) 01305 774074.*
Chairman: TBA.
Member Clubs: Clay Pigeon KC - Dunkeswell KC - Two Counties KC - Chasewater KC - Kent KC - Hoddesdon KC - Buckmore Park KC - Lincolnshire KC - Cumbria KC - Warden Law KC - West of Scotland KC - Cheshire KC - Manchester & Buxton KC - Camberley KC - Forest Edge KC.

North of Ireland Karting
Secretary: Mr K Wilkinson, 6 Innis Free Park, Newtownards, N Ireland, BT23 4AY. *Tel (h) 02891 814987; Fax 02891 822190.*

Wessex Kart Association
Secretary: Mrs C Bliss, 22 Flamingo Crescent, Worle, Weston Super Mare, Avon, BS22 8XH. *Tel 01934 511518.*

OTHER ADDRESSES

Association of Racing Drivers' Schools
43 King George Gardens
Broyle Road
Chichester
West Sussex
PO19 4LB   *Tel: 01243 789308*

Association of Racing Kart Schools
Stoneycroft
Godsons Lane
Napton
Southam
Warks
CV47 8LX   *Tel: 01926 812177*
email address: info@arks.co.uk
Web site: www.arks.co.uk.

British Kart Industry Association (BKIA)
Tudor Lodge
Belshaw Lane
Belton
Doncaster
DN9 1PF   *Tel: 01427 875900*
Fax: 01427 875455   *e-mail: impactpr@btinternet.com*

British Motor Racing Marshals' Club
Ballaugh
27 Dollicott
Haddenham
Bucks
HP17 8JL   *Tel: 01844 290631*

British Motor Sports Association for the Disabled
PO Box 120
Aldershot
Hants
GU11 3TF   *Tel: 01252 319070*

British Superkart Association
6 Mansfield Avenue
Quorn
Loughborough
Leics
LE12 8BD   *Tel: 01509 620702*

FIA (CIK)
CIK, c/o Federation International de L'Automobile FIA
Chemin de Blandonnet 2
1215 Geneve 15
Switzerland   *Tel: +41 22 544 4400*
Fax: +41 22 544 4450

194

Motor Sports Association
Motorsports House
Riverside Park
Colnbrook
Slough
SL3 0HG   *Tel: 01753 765000*
Fax: 01753 682938

8.4 USEFUL PUBLICATIONS

PUBLICATIONS AND TECHNICAL PAPERS AVAILABLE FROM THE MSA

Subject to availability the products and their prices are correct at the time of going to press but may be changed without further notice.

PUBLICATIONS (VAT zero rated)

MSA Competitors Yearbook	£20.00
MSA Kart Race Handbook	£3.00
MSA Officials Yearbook	£5.00
MSA Motor Sports Directory	£3.00
MSA Fixture and Clubs List	£3.00
MSA Starting Motor Sport	£3.00
FIA/CIK Kart Yearbook	£21.00
MSA Novice Kart Driver Pack	£31.00

TECHNICAL PAPERS

MSA Formula Cadet/TKM 2001 Chassis Homologation Book	£16.50
MSA Formula Cadet Comer S60 Engine Homologation Book	£10
MSA Honda GX160 Engine Specification Data Book	£10
MSA Gearbox Kart Engine Registrations Book	£5
MSA Formula 100c Liquid Cooled Engine Registration Book	£5

Amendments to above technical papers available on request with stamped, addressed envelope.

FIA/CIK Chassis and Engine Homologation Books can also be obtained from Karting Magazine (subject to availability). *Tel No: 01689 897123.*

Requests for the above with payment to: MSA, Motor Sports House, Riverside Park, Colnbrook, Slough, SL3 0HG.

MAGAZINES AND OTHER PUBLICATIONS

Autosport
The weekly magazine for the sport, covering national and international sport. Published every Thursday.
Haymarket Publishing, 38-42 Hampton Road, Teddington, Middx, TW11 0JE.

Tel: 020 8943 5000.

Cars and Car Conversions
A monthly magazine covering fast road and competition cars as well as some karting features. Includes lots of technical features and good information about getting started in motorsport.
Link House Magazines, Dingwall Avenue, Croydon, Surrey, CR9 2TA.

Tel: 020 8686 2599.

Karting Magazine
The best-established monthly magazine dedicated to kart racing.
Moorfield House, Moorfield Road, Orpington, Kent, BR6 OXD.

Tel: 01689 897123; Fax: 01689 890998.
email: support@karting-mag.demon.co.uk.

Karting Magazine Circuit Guide
The complete guide to driving on all UK (and some European) kart circuits, with a corner by corner narrative and accompanying diagrams.

What's on Motorsport Ltd, Newbarn Court, Ditchley Park, Chipping Norton, Oxon, OX7 4EX.

Tel: 01993 891000.

Motorsport News

The weekly newspaper for the sport, covering national and international sport. Published every Wednesday.
Motorsport News, Somerset House, Somerset Road, Teddington, Middx, TW11 8RU.

Tel: 020 8267 5385; Fax: 020 8267 5322.

Motor Sport

A monthly magazine, covering national and international sport with a particular emphasis on retro features.
Haymarket Publishing, 38-42 Hampton Road, Teddington, Middx, TW11 0JE.

Tel: 020 8943 5000.

Motorsports Now

The official publication of the governing body of British motorsport. Sent to all clubs and licence holders.
Motor Sports Association, Motorsports House, Riverside Park, Colnbrook, Slough, SL3 0HG

Tel: 01753 681736.

Racecar Engineering

A monthly magazine devoted to the engineering and technical side of motorsport.
Link House Magazines, Dingwall Avenue, Croydon, Surrey, CR9 2TA.

Tel: 020 8686 2599.

Racetech Magazine
A monthly magazine devoted to the engineering and technical side of motorsport.
4 Church Close, Whetstone, London, N20 0JU.

Tel: 020 8368 4121.

8.5 FLAG SIGNALS

The definitive description of flag signals will be found in the MSA 'Blue Book'. This should be consulted at all times.

The following flag signals may be displayed at the start/finish line:

Red flag: the race or qualifying session has been stopped. No overtaking.
Green flag: the start of a formation lap.
Black flag with orange disc and white number: there is a mechanical problem or fire on your kart that you may not be aware of and you must stop in the pits immediately.
Black and white diagonally split flag and white number: your driving is suspect and you are being observed. A second offence may lead to the black flag.
Black flag with white number: driver must stop at the pits within one lap and report to the Clerk of the Course.
Black and white chequered flag: end of race or qualifying session.
Black and yellow quartered flag: race neutralised, slow down and form up behind race leader. No overtaking.
Green flag with yellow chevron: false start.
National flag: race start (if lights fail). Note: In England this is the Union Jack but will vary for Scotland, Wales and Ireland.

The following flag signals may be displayed at marshals' posts around the circuit:

Red flag: the race or qualifying session has been stopped. No overtaking.

Blue flag (stationary): another competitor is following you closely.

Blue flag (waved): another competitor is trying to overtake you.

White flag: a slow moving kart or service vehicle is on the track.

Yellow flag (stationary): danger, slow down, no overtaking.

Yellow flag (waved): great danger, slow down considerably, be prepared to stop, no overtaking.

Yellow flag with red stripes: slippery surface.

Green flag: all clear at the end of a danger area controlled by yellow flags.

Black and yellow quartered flag: race neutralised, slow down and form up behind race leader. No overtaking.

8.6 GLOSSARY

ABkC	Association of British Kart Clubs
ARDS	Association of Racing Drivers' Schools
ARKS	Association of Racing Kart Schools
BSA	British Superkart Association
CIK	Commission International Karting
CoC	Clerk of the Course
FIA	Federation Internationale de l'Automobile
FMK	Federation Mondiale de Karting - predecessor to CIK
ICA	Inter-Continental A
JICA	Junior Inter-Continental A
MSA	Motor Sports Association
NATSKA	National Schools Karting Association
NDTC	Novice Driver Training Course
PF	Paul Fletcher International kart circuit

8.7 WEB SITES

GENERAL KARTING
Main UK karting site **www.karting.co.uk**
Another general site **www.kartingnews.co.uk**

ASSOCIATIONS AND RACE SERIES
Association of Racing Kart Schools **www.arks.co.uk**
Association of British Kart Clubs **www.abkc.org.uk**
British Superkart Association **www.superkart.org.uk**
210 Challenge **www.210challenge.fsnet.co.uk**
Club 100 **www.club100.co.uk**
FIA and CIK **www.fia.com**
Honda Challenge **www.ratpro.co.uk**
Motor Sports Association **www.msauk.org**
NATSKA (Schools Karting) **www.natska.freeuk.com**
Super One Series **www.abkc.org.uk/s1**
Super 4 Series **www.super4.co.uk**

CLUBS AND TRACKS
Bayford Meadow (Sittingbourne, Kent) **www.bayfordmeadow.co.uk**
Beccles (Suffolk) **www.bdkc.co.uk**
Buckmore (Chatham, Kent) **www.buckmore.co.uk**
Camberley (West of London) **www.ckc.globalspirit.net/**
Chasewater (North of Birmingham) **www.chasewater.krc.btinternet.co.uk**
Clay Pigeon (Dorset) **www.claypigeonkartclub.co.uk/**
Forest Edge (Hants) **www.fekc.co.uk**
Kingdom (Fife) **www.kingdomkartklub.co.uk/**
Larkhall (Hamilton, Strathclyde) **www.wskc.co.uk**
Raceland (near Edinburgh) **www.raceland.co.uk**
Shenington Kart Racing Club (Banbury) **www.sheningtonkrc.co.uk**
Whilton Mill (near Daventry) **www.whiltonmill.co.uk**

Kart Schools

ARDS (Three Sisters, Wigan) **www.aintree-racing-drivers-school.co.uk/**
Buckmore Park (Bill Sisley Kart School) **www.buckmore.co.uk**
Combe Karting (Castle Combe) **www.combe-events.co.uk/**
Deavinson (Ryehouse, Hoddesdon) **www.deavinsons.co.uk**
Protrain (Buckingham) **www.karttraining.co.uk**
Raceland (East Lothian) **www.raceland.co.uk**
Sandown Park (Surrey) **www.kartingatsandown.fsnet.co.uk**
Silverstone (Northants) **www.silverstone-circuit.co.uk**
SRS Racing (Hunts) **www.srsracing.co.uk**

Manufacturers and Traders

Anderson Karts (Yorks) **www.anderson-csk.co.uk**
Andy Cox Racing (Worcs) **www.andycoxracing.co.uk**
Andy Fairless Racing (Cumbria) **www.freezone.co.uk/afracing**
Biz Karts (Herts) **www.bizkarts.com**
Century Karting (Worcs) **www.century-karting.co.uk**
Deavinsons (Herts) **www.deavinsons.co.uk**
Grice Racing Engines **www.griceracing.com**
Jade Karts (Warks) **www.jadekarts.co.uk**
John Mills Racing (Worksop) **www.jmracing.co.uk**
Kestrel (Dunstable) **www.karts.co.uk**
O'Neill Racing (Slough) **www.oneillracing.com**
Parolin Karts (Devon) **www.parolin.co.uk**
Project One (Kent) **www.projectone-racing.co.uk**
Racesuits **www.gatellie.co.uk**
1st Racing Italian Karts **www.1stracing.co.uk**
Spellfame (Northants) **www.spellfame.co.uk**
Zip Kart (Herts) **www.zipkart.com**
Zip North (Manchester) **www.zipnorth.co.uk**

INTERNATIONAL LINKS
(Some of these are good for international race results and news)

German site **www.k-p-a.com**
'Original' (US) Kart Website **http://www.muller.net/karting/index.html**
Jesolo (Italy) **www.marconinet.it/jesolo/karting/**
Parma (Italy) **www.kartdromoparma.it/**
Planetkart **www.planetkart.com**
Sarno, Naples (Italy) **www.kartodromonapoli.com/**
Switzerland **www.kartverband.ch/trophee/index.html**
Vroom Magazine and News **www.vroom.it**